The Complete Guide to Writing Web-Based Advertising Copy to Get the Sale

What You Need to Know Explained Simply

D1224610

By Vickie Taylor

The Complete Guide to Writing Web-Based Advertising Copy to Get the Sale: What You Need to Know Explained Simply

Copyright © 2008 by Atlantic Publishing Group, Inc.
1405 SW 6th Ave. • Ocala, Florida 34471 • 800-814-1132 • 352-622-1875–Fax
Web site: www.atlantic-pub.com • E-mail: sales@atlantic-pub.com
SAN Number: 268-1250

ISBN-13: 978-1-60138-232-0   ISBN-10: 1-60138-232-4

Library of Congress Cataloging-in-Publication Data

Taylor, Vickie, 1984-
  The complete guide to writing web-based advertising copy to get the sale : what you need to know explained simply / Vickie Taylor.
      p. cm.
  Includes bibliographical references and index.
  ISBN-13: 978-1-60138-232-0 (alk. paper)
  ISBN-10: 1-60138-232-4 (alk. paper)
  1. Internet advertising. 2. Advertising copy. I. Title.

  HF6146.I58T39 2008
  659.14'4--dc22
                        2008025603

COVER & INTERIOR LAYOUT DESIGN: Vickie Taylor • vtaylor@atlantic-pub.com
PROOFREADER: Cathy Bernardy Jones • bernardyjones@gmail.com

Printed in the United States

Printed on Recycled Paper

*To Daddy, for telling me to dream my dreams,
and Mom, for helping me achieve them.*

Acknowledgments

So many people need to be thanked for helping me write this book. First, thank you to all the copywriters and business owners who took time out of their busy schedules to help me with this book. This book would not have been possible if not for you.

Second, thank you to my boyfriend, Michael, and to all my friends, for pushing me and pestering me to keep writing even when I did not want to. Though annoying at the time, your constant questioning on the status of my book helped me write it faster.

Third, thank you to every English teacher I ever had who encouraged me and told me to keep writing. A special thanks to two, Pam Bradley and Dava Tobey, who played significant roles in developing me to become a better writer and not settle for "crap." I appreciate your guidance and encouragement. Thank you for everything.

Table of Contents

Section 2: How to Write Copy for Various Online Media 77

Section 3: Where to Go From Here.... 257

Foreword

By Susan Greene
Copywriter

You have decided you want to be a copywriter. Now what? Where do you begin? How do you learn the craft?

How do you make the leap from an idea in your head to an impressive online marketing presentation, one that will attract visitors to your Web site and convert them into customers?

Fortunately, it is not quite as overwhelming as it seems. The Complete Guide to Writing Web-based Ad Copy to Get the Sale is your virtual instruction manual. Author Vickie Taylor will take you step-by-step through the process of creating and promoting a Web site.

You will soon realize that when it comes to purchasing products or services on the Web, most people do not care what company they buy from. They simply are seeking a solution to a problem. If you can persuade them through your Web site copy that your product meets their needs, then they will buy from you.

With that in mind, this book will teach you how to write Web copy that:

- Identifies your prospects' desires

- Engages them with your understanding of those needs

- Explains your solution

- Describes its features

- Highlights its benefits

- Overcomes any objections the prospects may have

- Builds your credibility as their best resource

- Persuades them to act now with clear instructions on how to proceed

At its most basic level, good Web site copywriting provides the facts. It has the exact information that your customers seek and ultimately compels them to take action.

You cannot just toss random content on your site like a basket full of clean laundry that needs to be sorted. Readers will not sift through the mess. The clutter, like the mound of disorganized clothes, becomes an overwhelming deterrent. At best it is pushed aside to be dealt with later or, more likely, in the case of a Web site, it is ignored completely as the visitor clicks off to search for another more concise Web site.

To be effective in your Web copy, you need to carefully organize the information, employing words and categories that make sense to the reader. Use topic sentences and limit each paragraph to one main idea. Provide the right amount of information, enough to satisfy the readers' questions, but not so much that they will be overwhelmed.

Clarity is key. So is the tone. Web site copy should be conversational, written as if the author were actually speaking one-on-one to the visitor. Use simple sentences. Informal, down-to-earth language and a friendly manner will connect with your reader. Let your personality shine through. Even humor has a role in work-related Web sites. Copy that reads like a college term paper, impersonal and pretentious, is boring, and it is a challenge to comprehend.

You will learn that visitors are impatient. They want pages to open instantly. They want results. They want to find the information they seek or do what they came to do as quickly as possible.

The most essential features and text should be placed in the easiest-to-find locations. Unnecessary clicks, extra steps, requests for personal information, and other actions need to be eliminated. Tasks should be streamlined.

Scanning is the norm. Visitors want to glean the essence of your pages often with a mere glance. Strip away all the filler content to create a clean, lean Web site that focuses on exactly what your customers care about. Graphics and photographs are appealing, but only if they complement the text. Be useful. Be functional. Be concise.

In *The Complete Guide to Writing Effective Web-based Advertising Copy*, you will learn some basic design guidelines to make your copy look as good as it sounds. The use of simple tactics such as incorporating white space to let your copy breathe, adding subheads to make your copy scannable, sprinkling bullets to catch the eye, and selecting the right color and font, will make your pages more readable.

The quality of a site's content influences your credibility. A well-designed Web site with authentic information creates a favorable impression and a positive image. When tastefully done, it enhances trust in the company.

Ultimately, the objective is to create a Web site that is truly customer-centric. It must speak the customer's language, not the company's. With compelling Web content, you will make more sales and build a stronger brand.

Good copy is a competitive advantage, but it is not enough. Now you need to get people to come to your Web site. After all, the most brilliant write-up on the Internet is useless if no one stops by to read it.

In *The Complete Guide to Writing Effective Web-based Ad Copy*, Taylor shows you different methods for getting your selling message in front of potential buyers. If prospects are not buying from you, most likely it is because they do not know about you.

How do you get the word out? How do you reach your best prospective customers without spending a fortune? The answer is multi-dimensional and involves a combination of pay-per-click advertising, Internet public relations, e-mail marketing, blogs, online social networking, cross promotions, and more.

Search Engine Optimization (SEO) should also be an important part of your marketing mix. Your site must be crafted so that it appears in the top listings of search engines for your main keywords. Effective SEO can help you achieve high rankings that bring in targeted traffic and steady profits.

While SEO sounds intimidating and something best left to programming geeks, the basis of SEO success is rooted in good copywriting. In this book, you will learn SEO techniques that will help your site rise to the top.

Whether you are writing one Web site to promote your business or you are looking to become a professional Web site copywriter who works for a variety of clients, The Complete Guide to Writing Effective Web-based Ad Copy will take you from curious novice to online marketing expert.

On a personal note, up until about 10 years ago, I made my living as a freelance print copywriter. I mostly wrote brochures, ads, and press releases for a diverse group of clients. Business was steady, and I had a constant stream of new customers coming to me via word-of-mouth referrals and advertising agencies that subcontracted my services.

Then, in 1998 I decided to focus on writing for the Web. At that time, this was a unique niche. Most Web copy was being written by print copywriters who had little comprehension of how the new medium differed from the old. Few books, if any, existed that explained the dynamics of writing for the Web, and SEO was a discipline yet to be defined.

Limited informational resources made learning the craft of online copywriting a challenge, one mastered mostly by trial and error, but it also meant that I had limited competition. Ultimately, it was a good niche to pursue, one that positioned me for success in the future.

Now, more than 10 years later, the landscape has significantly changed. Nearly every company, large and small, has a Web site, and many recognize the value of continually growing that site and keeping it current. Businesses also realize they must allocate a significant portion of their marketing budget to online channels.

Web copywriters are in high demand. Companies need their help in crafting home pages, product pages, subscription pages, e-mails to customers, blogs, articles for e-zines, and e-newsletters.

For copywriters, it is boom time like never before. The sooner you learn the skills of online copywriting, the faster you can grow your clientele and charge premium fees. The demand is great right now and poised to explode in the future.

While the need for copywriters who do direct mail, print ads, and the like still exists, the area of real opportunity is in writing for the Web. Now is the time to become an expert online copywriter.

By reading *The Complete Guide to Writing Effective Web-based Ad Copy*, you are taking the first step toward learning the craft of online copywriting. You are capitalizing on one of the most dynamic trends in marketing history. I wish you the best of success as you embark on your adventure into this exciting field.

Susan Greene

Freelance Copywriter

www.SusanGreeneCopywriter.com

Susan Greene has been a professional, freelance copywriter for more than 20 years. She works with a diverse clientele ranging from hospitality and professional service companies to high tech and industrial firms. Based in Orlando, Florida, her clients are located throughout the country.

While in previous years Susan primarily worked in print media — brochures, public relations materials, newsletters and ads — today she spends most of her time creating copy for websites and e-newsletters. She has a broad understanding of Internet marketing and search engine optimization as well as a conversational writing style that converts website visitors into customers.

Susan has a BS degree in journalism from Syracuse University and an MBA from Southern New Hampshire University. She can be contacted at Susan@SusanGreeneCopywriter.com.

Preface

"To me the greatest pleasure of writing is not what it's about, but the music the words make."
Truman Capote

Writing this book allowed me to take a more in-depth look at the creative side of the advertising world and learn the techniques of copywriting. It allowed me to further the knowledge that my bachelor of science (B.S.) degree provided me and to explore copywriting, a subject area with little focus at the University of Florida.

I have written advertising copy for several businesses, though I fancy myself a designer/art director rather than a copywriter. By researching and writing this book, I have gained a deeper appreciation for the other half of the creative world (writers) and have a better all-around knowledge of how the creative process works. Do not be disillusioned, but the creative world of advertising is tough stuff.

Through researching this book, I have learned tricks and tips about copywriting that I never knew before, many of these from professionals with years of experience. Now, I have the ability to share these techniques with you.

My hope is that you will learn what goes into advertising and how to develop a strategic, creative message that is targeted to your market. I also hope you will be able to profit from reading this book and take your product or service to the next level in sales.

Introduction

"Creativity is a type of learning process where the teacher and pupil are located in the same individual."
Arthur Koestler

Writing copy is not as easy as it may seem. Countless hours are spent researching and analyzing the situation before creativity ever plays a part. If you are fortunate, you will not be the one doing the research, just the one synthesizing it. It is up to you to take that information and craft it into a tangible medium that produces sales results. If you are one of those people who has to calculate the numbers on how effective your advertisement is, I offer you my sympathies.

As a new media, online advertising is constantly changing. Thus, this book is here to guide you on how to write the right words to get the sale online. It does not tell you which venue of online media is best for your business. It does not tell you how to calculate your return on investment (ROI), cost per thousand (CPM), cost per impression (CPI), cost per point (CPP), or any other acronym related to math and media planning. What this book does, however, is provide you with an outline of advertising and the basic principles of online advertising. It teaches you how to do proper research so that you know your consumer. It tells you which words are most effective and offers you hints, tricks, and suggestions from copywriters in the field.

What works and what does not work is up to you and your particular situation. Read the rules and feel free to break them. After all, that is the fun of being creative.

This book is divided into three sections. The first section familiarizes you with the research process and helps you understand what you need to know to develop successful Web copy. The second section shows you the various types of media you can write for on the Web and gives you tips and suggestions on how to write for each of them. The third section gives you suggestions on hiring a copywriter or finding a copywriting job.

So swallow your workday boredom, loosen your tie, and learn how you, too, can have one of the most fun careers in business — being a copywriter.

Section 1

Knowledge Is Power

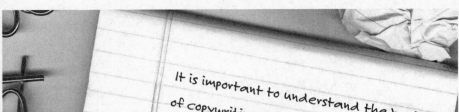

It is important to understand the basics of copywriting before jumping into writing. If you do not learn the rules, you will not know how to break them. To better read and understand this section, you may require a strong cup of coffee.

The first section of this book walks you through conducting the proper research to formulate your advertising problem, teaching you how to write a situation analysis and how important it is to know your target audience. Learn from basic examples of the fictional company Guac-n-Rock Guacamole. You will also discover the meaning of a creative brief, the benefits of writing one, and how to write one. Finally, this section teaches you how to be creative and what copywriting is all about, and it introduces you to the basic principles of copywriting.

Cop·y·writ·ing
[kop-ee-rahy-ting]

"Quantity produces quality. If you only write a few things, you're doomed."
Ray Bradbury

Copywriting

What do you get when you cross a writer with a salesperson? The answer is a copywriter. A copywriter writes words that encourage consumers to purchase items or services. It is a vital aspect in the grand scheme of marketing, because it is the part of the advertisement that communicates what you, as a business, wish the consumer to do.

If you have never written copy or taken a class on writing copy before, do not make the mistake of judging advertising from an outside perspective. It is easy to recall commercials that have made you laugh, such as the Citibank identity theft spots or the Budweiser talking frogs. If you want to watch funny commercials, you can watch the next Super Bowl, where the best creative advertising in the business is supposedly presented. However, the objective of advertising is not to be funny. Humor is a tactic that advertising uses for its ultimate objective — creating the sale. So do not think the hilarious advertisement you created that you think is Clio-Award worthy is necessarily effective.

Bright Idea

The objective of advertising is not to be funny. It is to drive a sale.

Skills Necessary to Copywriting

Do not think you have to be creative to be a copywriter. Although creativity helps, it is not everything. It is much more important in advertising to be effective. So often, the idea of being creative overrides the objective of selling. If you have the passion to make the sale, you can be ten times the copywriter of the most creative person in existence. This is because you have a basic understanding of the underlying principles of the job.

To become a better writer, it takes writing. Stephen King said, "If you work out with weights for 15 minutes a day, over the course of 10 years, you are gonna get muscles. If you write for an hour and a half a day for ten years, you are going to turn into a good writer." Find good copywriting. Visit good Web sites. Write this copy by hand over and over until you understand it. Then, try your own. There is no better way of learning than by doing.

To be a copywriter, it helps to have experience — plenty of experience — and not necessarily copywriting experience, although that may help. It helps to have a diverse background full of different activities that you can draw on when you are crafting copy. It is easier to write copy about surfing if you have surfed before. It is easier to write copy about guacamole if you have eaten it before. Since experiences create ideas, it is best if you can gain as much experience as possible in anything you are writing about.

You also must be tough. Not everyone will like what you do, and you have to remain strong enough to accept defeat. You have to be able to handle rejection. The first time I tried to write copy, it was different from anything I had ever written before, and it was thrown back in my face. I say this not to deter you from your copywriting endeavors but rather to caution you to others' acceptance of your work. You are going to craft some bad copy, perhaps even some horrible copy. What is important is to draw on that experience and understand how to succeed in the future.

Last, you must be a salesperson. That cannot be said enough. Sell. Sell. Sell. This is important to think about at every step in writing copy. You can get past the little stuff, like grammar, computer viruses, and the end of the world, if you just know how to sell.

The Work Arrangement

Ideally, a copywriter works alongside an art director, at least at advertising agencies. This pair forms a unique marriage. They help each other analyze a problem and create a solution. One often works on visual communication, while the other crafts the oral or written communication. The team members are able to play off each other's ideas to see what works best. Then, they take the advertisement they have crafted to the creative director and see how he or she likes the work. Then the team will go back to the drawing board; however, if the creative director is pleased with the advertisement, it will be presented to the client, where it will either pass or fail.

This is often not the case with small businesses. Not everyone has the luxury of a team in an organized system with inspection checks. If you are not in the agency, you are likely not going to be working as a team, and you are likely going to seek the approval of only your client or your boss, depending on the type of work arrangement you have. Because there may not be many people to work with (and those people you do work with likely will not know advertising), this means you need to know what you are doing — and know it well. You look much better if you produce a less colorful work that produces results than if you craft the cleverest advertisement that your client/boss has ever seen. The importance here is selling your work.

Have an understanding of why you created the copy the way you did, know that it will produce sales and why, and know how it is effective. You have to sell the ad to your creative director, and then the creative director has to sell the ad to the client. It is best to go into the meeting with hard facts backing up your point. Sell an ad that sells.

Thus, you begin to understand the importance of salesmanship. It is not just about what you write and how you sell that; you also have to sell your product to the client or company who is going to use it. Selling is a major facet of life for a copywriter.

The Most Basic Part of Copywriting: Words

Words are the most important part of any advertisement. Some people would argue that the image is more important; however, the image is there to catch the consumer's attention. For the consumer to know what the advertisement is about, he or she has to see and understand the words. The words can be only the name of the product; but, without knowing that, the consumer does not know what the advertisement is in reference to. Unless, of course, you have a large company, such as Nike, that is easily identified by its logo. In those cases, you do not necessarily need the words, because you have such strong brand recognition. However, most businesses do not have the luxury of high-brand recognition like Nike does; thus, the words in the advertisements tell the consumer what to purchase, why to purchase it, and where to purchase it. In summary, words drive the sale.

If your words fail to catch the reader's attention, you have failed. The most important part of copywriting is the first word. The second most important part of copywriting is the second word. Perhaps you can guess what the third most important part of copywriting is — the third word. Each word is there to keep the reader's attention and cause him or her to read onward. If at any point the audience's attention drifts elsewhere, you have lost the sale.

Copywriting for the Web is not much different from copywriting for any other medium. What differs is the amount of space you have to communicate your message. This does not necessarily mean that you should be long-winded or that you should cram as many words as possible onto your Web site or Web advertisement. This would be ineffective and pointless. Rather, you have as much space on the Web as it takes to write a comprehensive and cohesive message that keeps a consumer reading until it is time to make the sale.

Another part of online copywriting that is different from other media is that you can have hyperlinks embedded in your advertisement or Web site that link consumers to other pages. These are best placed in online advertisements to easily direct the consumer to your Web site. Then, you may choose to strategically place them on your Web site in key parts of the copy to help the consumer more easily navigate your site and find other related material. Finally, and most important, you want to have a hyperlink somewhere in your copy to direct consumers to the sale.

Bright Idea

No matter how fancy, cute, or clever you may be, selling is always the bottom line in business.

Case Study: James Palmer

What made you want to become a copywriter?

I have always wanted to be a writer, but I never bought into the "starving artist" mentality. Like many writers, I started writing fiction, then moved into nonfiction, and later, discovered copywriting. I learned that there are businesses that will pay writers good money to write their Web copy, press releases, direct mail, and corporate communications materials, and I knew that this was what I had to do.

Case Study: James Palmer

What was your first assignment? How did you feel about it?

My first assignment was a Web site for a freelance graphic designer. I was nervous at first. I was not sure if I could do a good job and give the client what she wanted. I had written online content at this point, including my own site, but I had never written Web copy for someone else.

What do you know now that you wish you had known when you first started?

I wish I had known more about the general aspects of running a business. Things I have had to learn through trial and error: effectively pricing my services, marketing myself, things like that.

What is the toughest copywriting challenge you faced?

I think finding clients and balancing career and family life are my toughest challenges.

How does Web copywriting differ from traditional copywriting?

With Web copywriting, you must remember that you are writing for a different medium. The same thing you would write for a brochure or a research paper is not appropriate for viewing online. You must break up the text into readable chunks. You also have to write so that search engines can find your content.

Who are some of the clients you have worked for?

I have written for copywriter Bob Bly; author and public relations (PR) consultant Jill Lublin; Early to Rise; and a wide variety of small businesses, coaches, consultants, entrepreneurs, Internet marketers, and other copywriters.

What is your biggest success? What copy have you crafted that you loved?

I just completed an online sales letter for an eBook that teaches small businesses how to start their own blogs. That is my best work to date. It was an interesting product, and I love the challenge of writing a good sales letter. They are just such fun pieces to write.

What are the best tips you have for successful Web copywriting?

1.   Write like your prospects talk.

2.   Break the text into easy-to-read paragraphs of no more than three sentences.

Case Study: James Palmer

3. Write benefits instead of features. Features are the physical aspects of your product: matte black carrying case, on/off switch, and so on. Benefits are what those things do for the consumer. Always think about how your company, products, or services benefit your prospects. No one cares that you have been in business since 1864 or that you are the industry leader in supply chain management software, unless those things help your customer in some way.

4. Have a goal for your Web site. Every page on your site should have a purpose. Think about what it is you want your prospects to do when they go to your site. Do you want them to request more information, order a product, download a white paper? Know what you want them to do, and then tell your prospect to do it.

Do you feel it is more important in copywriting to be creative or a salesperson?

I think you have to be a little of both. You must be creative when getting inside the prospect's head and writing in a way that makes them want to keep reading. You must be a salesperson when you are directing them toward a specific action, whether it be to click on a "Buy" button or give you their name and e-mail address.

What part of the Web do you find it easiest and hardest to write for (Web sites, banner ads, or e-mail) and why?

Web sites are the easiest for me to write. I am so familiar with the medium and I have been doing it so long, it is just easier for me to see what the final product should look like and suggest other ideas the client may not have thought of that would improve the site. E-mails are somewhat difficult because you must write them to make sure they stay out of the recipient's spam filter.

How do you succeed in writing Web copy?

If you are a copywriter doing it for a client, make sure you have all the information you need. Take a look at their current Web site, if they have one, look at their previous marketing materials, and learn everything you can about the company.

If you are doing it for your own business, check out what your competitors are doing and see if you can go them one better. Have a plan in mind. In other words, know how your site fits in with your business, your brand, and what you want the site to do for you. Do you want it to fulfill orders? Attract leads? Make a name for yourself? Do not just throw something up on the Internet because everyone else has a Web site too and expect amazing things to happen.

Case Study: James Palmer

What makes the Internet a great media for advertising?

The minimal expense involved and the fact that almost everyone has access to it and uses it every day.

Which companies do you feel do best by advertising on the Internet?

With the huge number of services available, including pay-per-click advertising and social media, plus the minimal expense, just about any company can be successful advertising on the Internet. Large companies are doing it, as are small businesses and entrepreneurs. The Internet is a great medium for those selling information products, but a company can do well with just about any product or service, as long as they have done their homework.

Freelance Business and Marketing Writer

www.jamesmpalmer.com

http://thecopywritingblog.blogspot.com

It Is All About the Business

"The general who wins the battle makes many calculations in his temple before the battle is fought. The general who loses makes but few calculations beforehand."

Sun Tzu

If you are not employed at an advertising agency, you may have to create a marketing plan (a subsection of the business plan). This gives you a better understanding of the underlying problem that the business faces. It also keys you in on the competitors, trends, and consumers. Even if you do not have to go through the process of researching this information, it is still important to know what to look for in it.

A key part to a marketing plan is the situation analysis. There are five parts to a situation analysis: company, product, consumer, market, and competition. Although they are all important in their own way, the three most important are market, competition, and consumer. These three areas give you the most insight into how to craft your copy in the most effective way.

The company and product analysis are simply that: They give all the details about the company and the product. These parts can be shorter than the others and often do not give you any real detail to the pressing issue at hand.

Competitive Analysis

Why make mistakes? Learn from your competitors. In this part of the situation analysis, you need to define who your competitors are. You can have direct and indirect competitors. For example, Guac-n-Rock Guacamole may have XYZ Guacamole and ABC Guacamole as its primary competitors; however, they may also find themselves competing with the salsa and ranch dressing industries. It is helpful to look at what the direct and indirect competitors are doing so that you are aware of what you are up against.

Here, you need to determine your competitor's market share and see how yours relates. Market share is the percentage of sales that a company has. If your competitors are successful, you need to find out why. Find out what they are doing that works. Then you need to find out how to make it work for you. Likewise, if your competitors are unsuccessful, determine why and make sure you do not do the same thing. Analyze the following list of factors:

- Where are they advertising?

- What do their advertisements look like?

- What else are they doing for marketing?

- How is their publicity?

- How do consumers perceive them?

- Where are their products located?

- How much do their products cost?

- How does their advertising read?

- What is their unique selling point?

- What are their sales for the previous year?

- Are their numbers increasing?

- What is their distribution?

- How is their quality?

- What is their reputation?

- How long have they been in business?

- Do they have a Web site?

- What is their Web site traffic?

You may come across other factors that need more analyzing, given your product or service's particular problem. Also realize that you may not be able to find answers to some of these questions because it may be proprietary information.

Bright Idea

Proper research helps you determine your problem and allows you to better assess your competitors.

Do not just dismiss the unsuccessful things your competitors are doing. Make sure you analyze these things and pay special attention to them. They save you the hassle of making the same mistake yourself, and you can find something that works better for you. Always think of what your company can do better and then execute the idea. Do not be afraid to take risks, especially in advertising.

In this digital age, pay special attention to your competitor's Web site. Since this is the portal that many consumers and potential consumers will visit, you need to know if your competitor's Web site is successful or not. If it is not, you need to pay particular attention to it and learn from it. What can you do to improve the quality of your Web site and pull consumers to your business?

Make sure you analyze your competitor's Web site thoroughly. Go beyond the text that you first see and view the page source code. You can do this by right-clicking (or control-clicking if you have a Mac) and selecting "view page source." This will clue you in on how the Web site was created, including key words that it uses to help its search engine results.

Always ask yourself what your competitor could do better. Why is its copy so poor, and what could you do to improve it? Or if its copy is stellar, ask yourself why and how you can replicate that within your copy. When you discover the answers, avoid the unsuccessful tactics in your copy and use the successful ones. Do not be afraid to try something different. Just because your competitor is going about business one way does not mean it is the right way. This is why you need to continue to analyze what it is doing. Check back with its Web site periodically to see what it is doing. Perhaps one time when you check it, you will see it has mimicked your style. If that happens, check the numbers for market share, because it realized that what you are doing works.

Market Trend Analysis

Market trends help determine the "next big thing." It is important to see what trends are in the market. As a copywriter, you should be aware of your surroundings, and you should be interested in what is going on in the world. If you were selling a food item, such as Guac-n-Rock Guacamole, it would be beneficial to know health trends. This may be a potential way to angle your copy to reach the consumers of your product.

These trends can vary by region or country. What is "in" in one area may be "out" in another. It is important to watch trends closely, not just from what you have established in your marketing plan, but on a day-to-day basis. In large advertising agencies, jobs are dedicated to analyzing market trends. Perhaps your budget does not allow for this luxury; however, keeping up with the news and observing your surroundings help you gain a better idea of trends. If you are on top of trends, you can gear your advertising copy to reach into the future. This helps your company capture market share.

Knowing the trends that are happening in various areas helps you craft your Web copy to fit one particular area. With Internet advertising, you are able to cater your advertisements to specific demographics or geographic sections. This helps you individualize the message of your product or service and makes your consumers think you are speaking directly to them.

Analyzing the market also helps you discover if there is a new need that can be filled by your product or service. For example, if Guac-n-Rock Guacamole determined that there is a need for a healthy, low-calorie burger topping, the business can easily provide that. It would need to educate consumers on this new use for guacamole and position it as a burger topping rather than as a dip. It would then, theoretically, increase its market share in the condiment industry as opposed to the dip industry and create a more versatile use for guacamole.

Consumer Analysis

Who are your consumers? The consumer analysis is quite possibly the most important part of the marketing analysis. It is vital to you as a creative to know your consumer. This is the person you must reach to sell your product. If you fall short because you fail to understand an aspect of the consumer, you should have studied him or her in more depth.

The consumer analysis should provide details on ways to reach the consumer. It should tell you what he or she likes and dislikes. It should tell you what is important to him or her, what he or she likes to watch on TV, and what the consumer is getting for Christmas (maybe only Santa knows that). You have to understand the consumer from the inside out.

One of the best ways to get into the mind of a consumer is to write a story about a day in his or her life. When you do this, be detailed and use lots of adjectives. Give this person a name, a job, a house, children, and more. Whatever fits, give it to your customer. List when this person wakes up, what he or she does first thing in the morning, what time this consumer drinks coffee (if he or she drinks coffee), and what time he or she goes to work (or if he or she is a student or unemployed). Take the time to get to know the consumer. If you do this, you can write effective advertising copy that reaches your target consumer at his or her most intimate levels.

For example, let us take the fictional brand Guac-n-Rock Guacamole. The company has determined through extensive market and sales research that its target consumers are women aged 24 to 34. Now, as a creative wanting to craft an advertisement to reach this target market, you have to understand them more in-depth than a generalized overview. By walking through a day in the life of one of the target consumers, you are able to glean useful information about how this person incorporates the product into daily life or see where the product can be more effectively incorporated.

Example of a "Day in the Life" Exercise

Susie Smith rolls out of bed every morning at 6 a.m. to the disruptive tone of her alarm clock. She rolls over and hits the snooze button in order to gain some much-needed shuteye. It goes off again at 6:10 a.m., and she once again hits the snooze button, proclaiming how she needs only five more minutes of sleep. Finally, at 6:20 a.m., she grudgingly gets out of bed. She yawns and stretches and then makes her way to the shower.

Susie kicks a shirt on the floor that is overflowing from her hamper. She reminds herself that she needs to do laundry soon. She gets into the shower and lets the hot water rush over her body. She stands there wishing she could fall back asleep and curses herself for staying out so late the night before.

Example of a "Day in the Life" Exercise

At 6:40 a.m., she emerges from the shower and quickly dries off and brushes her teeth. She tugs on her wrinkled dress pants and grabs one of the two remaining clean blouses from her closet. She swears that she will do laundry tonight.

At 6:50 a.m., she goes into her kitchen and grabs an energy drink from her refrigerator. The caffeine is welcome, as it will help her get a jump-start on what she already feels will be a long day at the office. She puts together a quick lunch of baby carrots and ranch dressing, a sandwich, and some chips — not a completely unhealthy meal but an inexpensive one containing the few things she has in her refrigerator.

She runs out of her house around 7:05 a.m., five minutes later than she needed to be. It means she will likely be five minutes late to work, depending on traffic. This is nothing unusual.

Traffic keeps stalling Susie on her way to work. She wishes that the person in front of her going 35 miles per hour in a 40 mph zone would speed up to 45. (She knows you can always get away with going five miles over the speed limit.)

She pulls into work at 7:59 a.m. and searches for a parking spot near her building but to no avail. She parks her car in what she thinks is the other side of the world and rushes into her office. She manages to clock in at 8:04 a.m. after her brisk walk, only four minutes late.

Her first stop is her desk. She drops off her purse and keys and turns on her computer. While it loads, she hurries off to the break room to pour herself a fresh cup of coffee, making sure to add plenty of creamer. She says hello to several of her coworkers before returning to her desk. When she gets back to her desk, she checks her e-mail and pretends to be working. She will not accomplish anything until at least 10 a.m. The first two hours, she will try to catch up on activities from yesterday and "work," which she defines in the morning hour as purchasing gifts online.

This is only the morning routine of Susie Smith. To create an effective "day in the life," you need to flesh out the rest of her day. What does she do at work? When does she get home? What does she do when she gets home? Does she decide to do her laundry?

When you are finished, go back through and ask yourself questions about what you have written. Some questions from the previous example might include:

- Why does Susie find the sound of her alarm clock "disruptive?"

- Why does Susie pack her lunch?

- Which brand of energy drink does she have for breakfast? Why?

- Why does Susie have so much laundry to do?

- Why are Susie's pants wrinkled?

- What did Susie do the night before?

- Why does Susie not work the first two hours of her job?

There are no right or wrong answers to these questions. They help you understand more about the consumer.

From Susie's morning routine alone, we can determine the following things:

- Susie is always in a rush (she is always late).

- Susie likes to add flavor to her food (ranch dressing and coffee creamer).

- She packs a somewhat healthy lunch (carrots, sandwiches).

- She has many loads of laundry to do (hamper overflowing).

She dislikes waiting (traffic, possible reason for not doing laundry).

From this, Guac-n-Rock Guacamole can determine a better way of positioning its guacamole product. Susie might enjoy smaller portions that are easy to take along with her for lunch. She would be pleased with a healthier alternative to flavor her vegetables or sandwiches.

Bright Idea

In writing effective advertising copy, knowledge is power.

The more you understand your target consumer, the better you can write. Often when you are writing a "day in the life of," you choose certain events by chance. When you analyze why you made these decisions, you gain more insight, which helps you understand the consumer.

SWOT Analysis

The SWOT analysis examines four key elements of your business — strengths, weaknesses, opportunities, and threats (SWOT). Each of these elements is composed of as many bulleted, detailed sentences as possible. This summarizes the situation analysis and helps prepare an outlook for your business.

When you analyze these different elements, you obtain insights into your business and the market around you. Ideally, these key you in on what your unique selling point (USP) is and also clue you in on what business problem must be solved.

Let us further build on the Guac-n-Rock Guacamole example by making a SWOT analysis chart.

Strengths

- ✎ The brand is all-natural and not packed with preservatives.

- ✎ The guacamole is chunky because it is made from real avocados.

- ✎ The guacamole tastes like real guacamole because it is made from avocados.

- ✎ Consumers like the taste of it compared to its competitors.

Weaknesses

- ✎ The brand is packaged in a box, which gives consumers the impression that the guacamole is not as good as guacamole that comes in containers.

- ✎ Guac-n-Rock has low distribution in grocery stores.

- ✎ Guac-n-Rock is located in the produce section, whereas its competitors are located in the dairy section, making it hard for consumers to locate.

Opportunities

- ✎ Consumers are becoming more health-conscious, and guacamole is healthy.

- Consumers like guacamole, but it does not often come to mind when thinking about dips.

- Guacamole can be used as a dip and a condiment on foods.

Threats

- Dips are impulse buys, so if a consumer is not thinking about purchasing one, he or she will not purchase it.

- Guacamole is not a dip on the forefront of consumers' minds.

- Consumers may prefer to make their own guacamole.

- Guacamole contains fat, even though it is a healthy fat.

Combining Everything to Create a USP

After looking over your situation and SWOT analyses, you should be able to better determine your brand/company's unique selling point, or unique selling proposition. This gives you a better direction on where your advertising is going and helps guide you creatively.

The USP is derived from what sets your company apart from the competition. Another way to think of this is, what do you have to offer consumers that your competition does not?

Guac-n-Rock Guacamole is different from its competitors because it comes in a box and is made with real avocados, whereas its competitors come packaged in a tub and are loaded with preservatives. Thus, its USP would be: Guac-n-Rock Guacamole is the brand of guacamole that is made from real avocados and comes in a box.

Other well-known USPs are:

- Timex is the brand of watch that takes a licking and keeps on ticking.

- Secret is the brand of deodorant that is strong enough for a man but made for a woman.

- Papa John's is the brand of pizza that is made with better ingredients.

When you combine these three analyses, you have a better understanding of where your advertising is going. You know better how to craft copy to reach the consumer. This all affects the way you present your creative advertisement, online and off.

A strong USP can carry the creative a long way. It helps detail what the advertisement needs to say about the company or brand. The creative is what sells the USP. For Guac-n-Rock Guacamole, the creative illustrates why being made from real avocados and coming in a box is a better choice for consumers.

Media Choices

Another important reason to know your consumer well is because it affects which media you use. This book concentrates on online media, but there are many choices to make here as well. Creating a Web site is much different from using Google AdWords or a banner advertisement on someone else's Web site.

These choices affect how to formulate your Web copy. Some media have more constrained space than others. Certain key words may work better than others in different types of media. Various techniques on how to craft copy for different venues is discussed in the second section of this book. However, here this book highlights the basic outline of media planning so that you can make better-informed media decisions on how to use your creative materials effectively. It does you no good to have great creative materials and no one see them.

In media planning, you are concerned with reaching the consumer as often as possible within the constraints of your budget. You need to know where your consumers are going online in an effort to better reach them and direct them to your Web site. This, again, goes back to knowing the consumer as in-depth as possible. You have to find the consumer and bring him or her to you.

It is better to place your advertisements where your target consumers are going rather than in a category that your product falls into. For example, Guac-n-Rock Guacamole, being a food product, may wish to advertise only at online grocery store Web sites, thinking members of its target market of 25- to 34-year-old women browse these Web sites. However, the target market is visiting **www.ivillage.com** and **Yahoo.com** more often than any other Web site. In this case, Guac-n-Rock Guacamole should advertise where the consumer is going, not where it thinks the consumer should go. It is of no benefit to a company to advertise on a Web site that gives them no return on investment; it is just a waste of money.

Bright Idea

Advertise where the consumer is going, not where you think the consumer should go.

Another reason in media planning to know your consumer is because you can better know what type of advertisements appeal to him or her. For example, you would not want to use pop-up advertisements when you know your consumers hate them. There is no need to annoy your consumer and make him or her have negative thoughts about your brand or business. Here, a more effective strategic solution may be to have your Web site only as a means to communicate with the consumer or to choose a less intrusive online media.

Integrated Marketing Campaign

Having an integrated marketing campaign is a benefit for your product or service. It helps tie all your advertisements across various media together and create a cohesive campaign that consumers can easily associate with your business, product, or service. Think of this as how your letterhead matches your business cards and envelopes. You want your print ads to look like your Web ads to look like your Web site.

This type of campaign allows for every element to be similar and relate to each other. This provides for better name recognition among consumers. They find it easier to relate each ad to your product and be reached more often.

Perhaps your headlines read the same or at least similar. Perhaps the look is the same by using the same font face or the same colors. This allows consumers to see your print ads and automatically associate them with your Web site, billboards, and TV commercials. An integrated marketing campaign allows you to obtain a higher reach and frequency, which causes your advertising to be more effective.

Case Study: Marte Cliff

What made you want to become a copywriter?

It is hard to put a finger on one defining moment. I have always loved to write, but turning it into a career evolved from things I was doing for other careers and interests.

I started writing advertising when we ran a grocery store, because I did not like the material we got from the distributor.

After that, I got into real estate and had to write ad copy for the houses, plus "farming" letters. Then I got a broker's license and had my own agency to promote, so I began writing a monthly newsletter, articles for the newspaper, and so on.

During that time I got a notion to bring the Fourth of July celebration back to our small town, so I joined the Chamber of Commerce and started pushing for it. They said fine, as long as I did it all. So I started writing news articles and promotions to raise money for fireworks.

Then a few of us got together and started an animal rescue. We had to promote that in order to get donations, and since I was the only one in the group who enjoyed writing, it was up to me.

About the time I realized that writing promotions for real estate had become my favorite part of the job, I got the American Writers and Artists, Inc. (AWAI) letter telling me that I could make a career out of writing. So I took the course, and then another course, and started studying. I sold the real estate agency, and after another year or two quit real estate to write full time.

What was your first assignment? How did you feel about it?

My first paid assignment was a series of farming letters for a Realtor in the office I had left. How did I feel? Scared to death. Writing for pay was a completely foreign idea.

What do you know now that you wish you had known when you first started?

Case Study: Marte Cliff

Several things:

1.   Even the major names in copywriting receive criticism and revision requests from their clients. Do not take it personally.

2.   When you price your work too low, you label yourself an amateur.

3.   Never write anything without a signed contract and a deposit up front.

4   Always insist on the client giving you the background materials you need before you put fingers to keyboard. Those "Oh, I forgot to tell you's" can add days to a simple letter.

5.   Some people with letters and Web sites that are terrible like them that way. They will not turn into clients. Do not waste time on them.

6.   Friends and family will not understand that you are working. They will think that since you are at home, you are not doing anything, so it is all right to stop to visit or ask you to run their errands. You have to learn how to set limits.

What is the toughest copywriting challenge you faced?

In terms of writing the copy, it was a 15-page Web site rewrite for an interfaith seminary. For one thing, their terminology was foreign to me — and dictionary definitions were of little help in applying their interpretations and nuances to different words.

In terms of a continual challenge, it has to be pricing. Trying to determine how long a particular project might take is difficult. In addition, the temptation to lower my fees for a new business with an interesting project is strong. I have to remind myself that I cannot work for peanuts, no matter how much fun it might be.

How does Web copywriting differ from traditional copywriting?

I think it differs little. The same principles apply to a sales letter in the mail as a sales letter on the Web. I think that sometimes on the Web people try to say too much at the same time, which is a mistake that confuses their prospects.

You have to be aware of key words, but you should be aware of them in any sales letter, because those are the words that will show prospects you have what they seek.

Aside from that, the Web does offer the opportunity to give more and to form a relationship with your customers, so you create more pages of different kinds of copy.

Case Study: Marte Cliff

Who are some of the clients you have worked for?

Numerous Realtors, since my background leads me in that direction. A few animal rescue groups, for the same reason. A few of the others are Mouse House Tours,

Rockwater Properties, Property Loss Consultants, The Lands Council, The Association of Certified Anti-Money Laundering Specialists, Renu Herbs, Feel Bach!, Lifetime Optometry, and Nye Viking, Inc. I have also gotten slightly into the political arena by writing press releases and articles for Lewis Rich, a local county commissioner candidate (and yes, we won).

What is your biggest success? What copy have you crafted that you loved?

Because I write primarily for smaller companies that do not track results, I cannot quote ROI on my work. Writing for the Web, creating "drip e-mail" campaigns, and submitting press releases and articles is different from copywriting for direct marketing packages that either return money on the spot or not.

So, aside from fund-raising letters that came in when I was part of the organization and could track the results myself, I do not know which of my pieces has been most successful in terms of money.

I was rather pleased with a letter I wrote that brought in a 12 percent response to help homeless dogs.

I cannot say I have truly loved any of my copy. Even after I submit it, if I go back and look, I can see more changes I would like to make. There is always room for improvement.

What are the best tips you have for successful Web copywriting?

Remember that the top of the page is all important. Do not waste space on the company name. Instead, get a compelling headline out there to stop your prospects within three seconds. If people do not instantly see that you have what they are looking for, they are not going to search the page to see if it is there.

Get right to the point. Tell them you are going to provide the service they need or offer the products they want. After that, your copy can compel them to read on to learn how you will do it.

Be clear and use ordinary words. Forget industry jargon, unless you only want to appeal to industry professionals. Do not use a bunch of initials and expect that your visitors will know what they mean. "Utilizing the PGQ" may make perfect sense to

Case Study: Marte Cliff

you, but will be perfect nonsense to your visitors. And, above all, do not try to impress anyone with your vocabulary — you will only confuse people and cause them to go somewhere else with a more straightforward approach.

Offer plenty of white space, bold subheads, and bullet points. Reading on the Web is harder on the eyes, so make your paragraphs shorter, and write with the knowledge that many of your readers will be skimming the page, looking for points of interest.

If you are selling something, ask for the order, and explain how to buy. Do not ask your visitors to figure it out like a puzzle. They will not. And do not ask them to visit some other page to find the price — that is just rude and annoying.

Remember your key words. Be sure to use one or two of the primary key words in the headline and/or the first paragraph. Then sprinkle them throughout your copy — but only use them in places where they will naturally fit with the flow of the copy.

Do you feel it is more important in copywriting to be creative or a salesperson?

Be a salesperson — use your creativity to craft a message filled with benefits to the reader and a strong reason why they should take action.

What part of the Web do you find it easiest and hardest to write for (Web sites, banner ads, or e-mail) and why?

Web pages are easiest, because you have the benefit of space — although, as in any writing, you should strive to cut out unnecessary words and get right to the point of your message. You have the benefit of subheads and bullet points to draw the reader through and keep even "skimmers" interested.

E-mail is slightly harder, because you first need to get the message opened with a subject line that stands apart from all the junk mail we all get. Then you have to hurry and show that your message will be worth reading. I do not do banner ads but have to say that Google AdWords are the toughest. Getting a compelling reason why into those few words can take more work and time than writing several pages of ordinary copy.

How do you succeed in writing Web copy?

The same as with any copy. Preparation, hard work, and going back over it again.

What makes the Internet a great media for advertising?

You are talking to people who already have an interest in what you offer — and, of course, the price is right. Well-written Web copy can keep on working for you month after month — and it is there 24 hours a day. That is far different from a newspaper

Case Study: Marte Cliff

or magazine ad — or from a direct mail piece that is likely to land in the hands of the wrong person, even though you spent many dollars sending it.

I love the concept of letting your customers opt in to getting more messages from you, so you can then send e-mail promotions directly to people who want them. What could be better than presenting offers to people who already know and love you?

Which companies do you feel do best by advertising on the Internet?

I cannot think of any company that should not be on the Internet. There is no better way to tell your story and to let prospective customers learn who you are and what you offer. You can create trust and loyalty by offering informative articles and help; you can answer their concerns with a question-and-answer (Q&A) page; you can let them know you are a real person through your "about me" page; you can give detailed instructions about how to find your place of business; you can fully explain your services — the list goes on and on.

Even companies who do not sell directly through an Internet site can create a relationship with customers through the information given there. Then, if they add an option for their customers to sign up to receive special promotions and "Internet only" coupons to use in their retail stores, they are going one step further by letting that group of customers feel special.

The Internet presence and contact information also offer customers an easy way to communicate so that business owners can learn what their customers like and dislike about their products and services. This alone can be a valuable business-building tool.

*Marte Cliff is a freelance copywriter who specializes in Web copy, e-mail campaigns, sales letters, and press releases. Marte views the opportunity to learn and write about a variety of products and services one of the major benefits of a freelance career. However, due to her background as a successful real estate broker, she does write extensively for real estate and related businesses. She offers free marketing ezines and reports on her Web site at **www.marte-cliff.com**. Contact her by phone at 208-448-1479 or at writer@marte-cliff.com.*

The Creative Brief

"You can always spot a well-informed man —
his views are the same as yours."
Ilka Chase

A creative brief is a shortened version of your situation analysis that you use to develop your creative work. This document becomes a road map for you, because it details everything you need to know in a short outline.

You want to make sure that you receive a creative brief instead of the full situation analysis or nothing at all. The reason is because you need this roadmap laid out before you in a succinct manner. A situation analysis is too lengthy; you only need the pertinent information. Plus, what the business considers vital information may not be what you consider vital information. Thus, it is great to have a guide.

Bright Idea

Only a novice creative person goes into an advertisement blind. Make sure you know the guidelines before you start crafting your advertisement, or you may find that you have wasted your time.

If you prepared the situation analysis and you are also doing the creative work for your company, developing a creative brief may also be a good strategy for you. A creative brief helps you prepare your thoughts in a way that works best for your advertising campaign. You will be able to thumb through a one- or two-page document rather than your 30-page situation analysis, which will save you time.

If you are doing the creative brief for your company, keep in mind that there are many different creative briefs, and no one in particular is best for any company. You must decide what works best for you. You may find it helpful to look at other companies' briefs, if possible, to gain ideas on how to develop yours. This can be a fluid document. Just because you create one for your first project, does not mean it needs to be the same for your next project. If you find a new question or idea that you want to incorporate, do so.

A basic creative brief should contain the following:

1. **The background of the company and the big picture** — This part of the brief should sum up the

company, product, and market analysis in a few short sentences. It helps give the creative an idea of the market and the challenges the company is facing.

2. **The purpose for advertising** — This part tells the creative why you want to advertise. It is important because it defines your business' problem. Without defining the problem, the creative does not know exactly what he or she needs to accomplish through the advertising, and it can lead to bad or ineffective advertising.

3. **The objectives for advertising** — This part details what you hope to accomplish with the advertising. If you want to increase sales of your product by 5 percent over the next six months, this is where you need to say so. Perhaps you want only to increase awareness of your product. Different objectives cause the creative to use different strategies in creating your advertisements.

4. **The target audience** — Again, defining your target audience and knowing it is important. Here, list as many details as you know about the target audience. Give the creative a good picture of who these people are and what they like to do. This is vital in creating the advertisement for your company. The more the creative knows about the consumer, the more accurate and effective the advertising will be.

5. **The most important thing you want to say** — You have done the research, and you know what the pressing issue is. Again, tell the creative what the issue is and what you think is the most important solution/thing to say. You are

not writing your advertisement but giving the creative guidance on how it is to be written. If the most important thing to say for Guac-n-Rock Guacamole is that it is a dip and a condiment, then the creative will come up with a new solution on how to rephrase this and make it effective.

6. **Supporting evidence** — This tells the creative that there are things to back up what you think is the pressing problem. The supporting evidence influences what the body copy of the advertisement says, because it tells consumers why they should purchase the product.

7. **Mandatory elements** — This can be your logo, any trade characters that you have, or your slogan. This is whatever must be included in the advertisement. If you have visuals, such as your logo, you need to provide this material in a high resolution to your creative so that he or she can use it.

8. **Types of media to be used** — Again, crafting an advertisement for a newspaper is different from writing a TV script. It is helpful for the creative to know which media will be used in the campaign. Make sure you can also provide the creative with spatial constraints if you are using print or Web advertisements, as well as a time length for radio, TV, or Web video advertisements. It would be a waste of time to create an ad for a Web banner that is 468 by 60 pixels when you are going to be using a pop-up advertisement that is 336 by 250 pixels.

Sample Creative Brief for Guac-n-Rock Guacamole

Background of Company: Guac-n-Rock Guacamole has been around since 1987, started by Bob Smith. Bob wanted to create a healthy, great-tasting guacamole to be sold in grocery stores, so he developed a special process called Fresh Keeping to be able to help his guacamole retain the taste of pure avocados and keep it on the shelves longer.

Purpose for Advertising: Guac-n-Rock does not have the same amount of name recognition that other leading guacamole brands do. We want our consumers to associate Guac-n-Rock Guacamole as a fun, light-hearted brand they can use at parties and other social occasions.

Objectives for Advertising: We want to increase awareness of our product by 20 percent among our target audience over the course of the next year.

Target Audience: Our target audience is women aged 25 to 34. These women are rushed in their day-to-day lives. They often do not have time to prepare a full meal and need a quick and easy way to add flavor to their food. They are concerned about health but often find health food does not taste as good as other food or is too expensive. They like to have fun and enjoy the company of their friends. They often spend their free time on the Internet rather than watching TV or reading the newspaper.

Most Important Thing to Say: We want these women to know that Guac-n-Rock Guacamole is a fast and healthy way to add flavor to boring food. It can be used as a dip and a condiment.

Supporting Evidence: Focus studies revealed that guacamole does not come to the forefront of consumers' minds when they think of a dip or a condiment. They revealed that they do like guacamole and will use it if given the option, but they will not think of it on their own. They like to use guacamole on a variety of foods. Most see it as healthy, although some find it a little fattening, but they do recognize it as a good fat.

Mandatory Elements: We want our logo on the advertisement somewhere and on our Web site.

Types of Media to Be Used: We are using 15- and 30-second radio spots. We are also using Web advertising in the following dimensions: 300 by 600 pixels, 468 by 60 pixels, and 250 by 250 pixels. We would also like T-shirt designs and an overhaul of our current Web site.

Make sure you keep the creative brief on hand. Having this document can help you better assess the effectiveness of your campaign later. You may decide that you want to use the creative brief again, or you may determine that it needs to be revised for the future.

Case Study: Mike Spanjar

What made you want to become a copywriter?

I discovered creative writing in high school. I loved writing short fiction. By the time I reached my senior year, I thought about majoring in creative writing in college. My guidance counselor suggested I might want to specialize in something more "life-sustaining." We discussed other writing disciplines, and I came to realize that I really enjoyed the idea of copywriting. But at the age of 18, I had never heard of it before.

What was your first assignment? How did you feel about it?

I had been writing in the marketing department of a major local newspaper for years, but I consider my first assignment to be the first freelance project I took on. It came from a creative design firm. They needed copy for a Repel (insect repellent) ad. I remember feeling as though I had been thrust into this big, new industry. Suddenly, I was working for this awesome creative firm and writing for a national brand.

I can laugh now at how I handled the price negotiation. I had no idea what I was worth, and I was afraid to ask for too much money. I called a friend who was in the business and asked her for advice. She said, "Do not come in cheap. They will not respect you or your talent." She gave me a broad range to shoot for.

In the end, I did something beyond my years: I let the employer come up with a price. Bear in mind, it was the early 90s, so this will sound bad by today's standards. I was thinking of coming in at somewhere between $30 and $50 for the two and a half hours I spent on the Repel job. One of the principals said, "We were thinking that for projects this size, we would give you $140. Will that work?" I summoned every muscle in my body to contain my excitement and said, "Sure, that is fine." They wrote me a check on the spot. I could not wait to run home and show it to my wife. I was stunned.

Case Study: Mike Spanjar

What do you know now that you wish you had known when you first started?

Writing is a creative talent. It is amazing how few people can write compelling, inspiring copy — and understand the mechanics. When I started in this business, I thought everyone could write. That is the kind of mentality that makes young writers sell themselves short. If you are good at what you do, charge accordingly. Do not worry about the thousands of anonymous writers on the Internet selling their skills at two bucks an hour. There are plenty of companies who know those "writers" are charlatans and would rather pay top dollar for top talent.

What is the toughest copywriting challenge you faced?

It is something I face every day: juggling every project and delivering on time. Any contractor needs to know when to say "no" to someone when there are more assignments than hours in the day. I still have a real problem with that because, as a freelancer, I want to make sure the work keeps coming. Consequently, I regularly get less than four hours of sleep each night.

How does Web copywriting differ from traditional copywriting?

Traditional sales literature is often sent out by a salesperson to a prospect. The salesperson has the advantage of knowing who the prospect is or, at the very least, how to contact him or her. After a day or two, the salesperson can make a follow-up call and close the deal.

Web surfers are price shoppers; they are attempting to make purchasing decisions based on their own online research. They assume they will be able to determine what group of products suits their need and all they need to do is narrow the choices down to the best price. This empowers them. Web writers need to understand this behavior and use their best skills to compel these prospects to take some action that will get a salesperson involved or else seal the deal right then and there. The Internet, good or bad, has commoditized free trade and all but sidelined the salesperson.

Who are some of the clients that you have worked for?

My higher-profile clients include Harley-Davidson Motor Company, Master Lock, and FujiFilm.

What is your biggest success? What copy have you crafted that you loved?

It is difficult to pinpoint any one job. But if I had to identify one that I loved, it would be a self-promotional piece I created for a company I worked for. Not only did I write the copy, but the project was my concept, and I performed the design. The central

Case Study: Mike Spanjar

piece was a four-page menu format that appeared as though it came right out of a '50s diner. The copy was playful but informative. I was able to inject some of my dark humor throughout. My ego got a boost when the package was featured in a trade magazine due to its unique execution.

What are the best tips you have for successful Web copywriting?

Look at what the big players are doing. Imitation may flatter, but it also guarantees you will be on the right track. Read all you can about effective Web marketing, online shopping habits, and so on. Become an "expert." When talking with someone who might hire you to do creative work, you want to sound confident and knowledgeable about this unique market.

Do you feel it is more important in copywriting to be creative or a salesperson?

You need to be both, without question. Creative Web copy that does not sell the reader on a concept (this is a great product, service, company, idea, or whatever) is worthless. Even if the copy is not intended to sell a product, something is being sold, such as reputation or an experience. Likewise, copy that just goes for the jugular to get a sale will send visitors packing. As is true in any sales process, creative language will guide prospects right where you want them.

What part of the Web do you find it easiest and hardest to write for (Web sites, banner ads, or e-mail) and why?

E-mail is the most challenging assignment. It all boils down to the e-mail's subject line. What words can you use to get past the spam filters and compel a person to click on your message rather than delete it along with ten or so other unsolicited messages? This is truly an art. Every other form of Web writing is, in my estimation, "easy" by comparison.

How do you succeed in writing Web copy?

Like any good salesperson (and that is what you are when you freelance), ask questions of your customer and listen, listen, listen. Learn about their needs, their products, their competition, and so forth. The discovery process is similar to any marketing delivery system. Execution is another thing, and that goes back to understanding how to compel people to take action rather than leave. Be unusually creative, even crafty. On one of my freelance sites, I point out to the reader that they have reached the bottom of the page, and that if they have read it all the way to the bottom, I was successful at capturing their attention. It is difficult to imagine a would-be employer who would not think at that point, "Wow, that is exactly what I want visitors to do at my site."

Case Study: Mike Spanjar

What makes the Internet a great medium for advertising?

First, it is inexpensive compared to all other media. Second, it has the broadest reach — almost everyone in the world. Third, it is interactive — a company can engage visitors with pop-ups, surveys, games, multimedia, and other requests for input and participation. Last, it is part of this generation's life style. We depend on the Internet for so many things that consumers continue to look to the Web to make purchases or purchasing decisions.

Which companies do you feel do best by advertising on the Internet?

There is no good answer. The Web is equally effective at selling consumer products, (such as **amazon.com**), as it is selling advance movie tickets, flowers, novelty T-shirts, or automobile tires.

Mike Spanjar is a freelance copywriter who lives in Glendale, Wisconsin, a suburb of Milwaukee. A veteran writer of advertising and marketing copy, sales letters, feature articles, and search engine optimization (SEO) content, he began his career in 1986.

www.mikesmycopywriter.com

www.copywritermike.com

mikes@mikesmycopywriter.com

How to be Creative

Think you are uncreative? Think again. Not everyone can sit down and quickly come up with a stellar advertisement — not even the pros. The key to being creative and coming up with good material is to keep practicing and thinking.

Put the Pen to the Paper

A good way to start writing an advertisement is to take every idea you have swirling about in your head and write them all down. Do not stop writing until you have emptied your brain and cannot think of anything else to write. Once you have done this, take the sheet that you have spent the past few hours writing and throw it away.

It is often all bad. You may think you have just unlocked the secret to a great advertisement, but, in reality, you have not. If you came back to it in a few days, you would realize that everything on the list was bad for one reason or another. Perhaps it is too cheesy; perhaps it does not convey the real issue at hand. No matter the reason, nine times out of ten it will fall into the trash category.

Now you may be wondering what to do because every idea that you could think of was on that sheet of paper. Breathe. It is all right. You will think of more ideas — better ones. By getting these poor ideas out of your system, you are able to concentrate better on the task at hand and create advertisements that will help solve the business problem and appeal to the target consumer, rather than something you find to be good.

Reference the Pros

If you are still having a mental roadblock, try finding other advertisements. Determine why they are good or bad.

I find it good to have a reference library. Any time I come across a good advertisement, I clip it, make a copy of it, or take a screen shot of it and put it in a folder. This way, I can always come back to the folder for ideas. I am not suggesting you steal someone else's ideas but rather find inspiration in those ideas to develop your own work. This is great if you cannot think of a clever headline.

Someone else may have thought differently than you (and likely did), and you can see that and realize you have been going in the wrong direction.

Bright Idea

Have a collection of advertisements that you can turn to for ideas when you get writer's block.

If you do not have a collection of advertisements that you have been hoarding away in a large box in your closet, you can always surf the Internet to find advertisements. A good stop would be **AdWeek.com** or **AdAge.com**, but if you do not have a subscription, you can always try a Google image search. You may not come up with the best selection of advertisements, but it is a fun way to see how other people think of a particular situation.

Here is a list of places on the Internet that have collections of advertisements you might find useful to sift through for ideas:

- **AdAge** (**http://adage.com/century/campaigns.html**) — This Web site lists Ad Age's Top 100 advertising campaigns of all time. These are successful campaigns from all media. There are several links so that you can see the campaigns. Others you may have to search on Google to see.

- **Get It In Writing Blog** (**www.getitinwriting.biz/ blog/2007/04/amazing-advertisements_678.html**) — This blog has examples of great advertisements found around the world. It can help spark new and innovative ideas from what you might have otherwise thought were boring and mundane.

- **Sulekha** (http://cyco.sulekha.com/blog/post/2006/12/award-winning-advertisements.htm) — Pictures of award-winning advertisements from around the world.

- **Carbonmade** (www.carbonmade.com/portfolios/?tag=Advertising) — Links to portfolios of those in the advertising world. Since anyone can post a portfolio, the good advertisements come along with the bad advertisements. Sift through these for new ideas.

- **The Webby Awards** (www.webbyawards.com/webbys/current.php?season=11) — This Web site takes you from current winners back to 1997. These winners have all displayed the best Web sites on the Internet in various categories.

Work Your Brain

Another way to find and build your creativity is by using creative aerobics. This is a four-part technique developed by Dr. Linda Conway Correll. It allows your left brain and your right brain to work together to produce great advertisements. A benefit about the exercise is that you can do it without breaking a sweat. You can find out more about how to use creative aerobics in her book *Brainstorming Reinvented*.

The technique helps anyone who feels uncreative to develop strong advertisements. You can use the analytical left brain to help the creative right brain. This technique is good for those who need an extra push in thinking creatively or in finding a new way to sell a product.

Start by writing down everything you know about your product or service. Try to incorporate the five senses: sight, taste, smell, hearing, and touch. Make the list as long as possible so that you can incorporate everything you can think of. The longer the list, the more you can use later to write your advertisement.

Guac-n-Rock Guacamole will again be used as an example in all four steps of the creative aerobic process.

Step 1

Step 1 is taking facts about a product and writing them down. You will write down the physical facts, the learned facts, and the more creative facts.

Step 1: What we know about Guac-n-Rock Guacamole:

- It is made from avocados.

- It tastes like real guacamole.

- It is green.

- It is chunky.

- It comes in a box.

- It is mushy.

- It is wrapped in a plastic bag.

Part 2 of Step 1 includes taking apart one of the facts and writing down more facts based on it. For example, we will take the fact that guacamole is made from avocados.

Facts applied to avocados:

- They are sort of round.

- They have a reddish-brown pit.

- They are green.

- They are hard on the outside.

- They are soft on the inside.

- They have a skin.

- They are a fruit.

- They are darker on the outside and lighter on the inside.

- They grow on trees.

- They can be eaten.

- They are healthy.

You can continue to build lists off your first list. Then, if you wish to build more lists, you can build those off each additional list. Though this may seem silly at first, it will help supply you with more ideas.

Step 2

Step 2 requires you to come up with new names for your product. This is the step that starts to bridge your left brain to your right brain and cause you start thinking more creatively. This step will have you list nouns that are related to your product. The objective is to discover new names for your product that you would not have otherwise thought of.

For example, take the fact that guacamole is green, and write a list of ten nouns that are also green.

Things that are green:

- Grass

- Grapes

- Leaves

- Frogs

- Broccoli

- Cactus

- Emeralds

- Limes

- Cucumbers

- Shamrocks

- Aliens

From this list, you will pull a word and then create a new list of things associated with this item that are not associated with guacamole.

For instance, let us take the word "aliens."

Nouns connected with aliens:

- Mars
- Martians
- Anal probe
- Come in peace
- Spaceship
- Technology
- Foreign
- Outer space
- Conspiracies
- Skin
- Antigravity
- Unknown
- Weapons
- Movies
- Fiction

Now look at the facts generated about aliens and try to connect them with guacamole. For example, you can relate "unknown" to the ingredients that other guacamole brands use. You can also talk about the technology of the process used to make Guac-n-Rock Guacamole. If you go through each different word, you will collect a long list of phrases. Some words you will not be able to find an association with guacamole; others you will. This exercise helps stretch your word association and begins to effectively work your right brain.

Step 3

The third step is a bit trickier than the previous two. We have already begun working on the process of Step 3 at the end of Step 2. Here, you will take a word generated from your first fact list and pair it with a word from the second. You are concentrating on two dissimilar objects to find the creative similarities between them. Though this may sound a bit absurd, it can generate some creative results.

For example, let us find the similarities between that of a box (what the guacamole comes in) and skin (a word that we associated with aliens).

Step 3: It comes in a box and they have a skin:

✎   Both are used for protection.

✎   Both can be smooth.

✎   Both can have art on them.

✎   Both can be torn.

✎   Both can have holes.

Both can be touched, seen, tasted, and smelled.

Step 4

The fourth and final step is creating new definitions for two-word phrases or common sayings. This involves two activities: coming up with the phrase and then defining it. Here, we make a new list that relates to the other lists. The object is to come up with two-word phrases or sayings that describe the product, and then give those two-word phrases a new definition. These words may come from other words that you have previously put down. An excellent way to find these phrases is to pick up a copy of a dictionary and look up a word. In the definition, there will be common phrases the word is used in.

To help clarify this exercise, an example might be that of a serial killer. If we change the serial to its homophone, cereal, then a new definition might be someone who eats an entire box of cereal in the morning. The point of this exercise is to write headlines that grab the attention of the consumers and make them think differently about the product. This step gives you a headline for your advertisement; your body copy further explains the headline.

This step is often the most difficult, but it is also the most rewarding. You need to come up with as many definitions as possible so that you have an ample amount to choose from. An ideal number is at least 20. You will find that some of your definitions work and some of them do not.

Step 4: Phrases

 Green with Envy

- Green Peace/Piece

- Hole in One

- Skinny Dipper

Step 4: Definitions

- **Green with Envy:** All other foods are jealous of those foods coated in guacamole.

- **Green Peace/Piece:** Guacamole is mashed-up pieces of avocados that help save bland food.

- **Hole in One:** Your mouth is a winner every time you buy Rock-n-Guac Guacamole, the guacamole that has a hole in the box.

- **Skinny Dipper:** Someone who dips his or her chips in healthy guacamole.

You can see that not all these definitions work easily with the product. The best two would be Green with Envy and Skinny Dipper. Both of these would easily grab the consumer's attention and cause him or her to read your advertisement. With Skinny Dipper, you can remember that sex sells, but your advertisement does not necessarily have to be sexy.

By using the four-step creative aerobic process, you can have lists of ideas to use for your advertisements. The best part is that anyone, creative and non-creative alike, can use this workout to develop ideas. If you find common themes, you can create a cohesive campaign.

Although creative aerobics are not for everyone, some people can effectively use them to become more creative and develop ideas they would not have otherwise thought of.

Get Inspired

To become more creative, you can be inspired by other aspects of your life. Here is a list of simple suggestions that may jog your creativity:

Take a hike. Instead of sitting in the office, waiting for inspiration to strike, go for a walk. This helps clear your mind and allows you to focus once you get back to the office.

Sketch it out. Instead of writing down ideas, try drawing pictures. Pull out the crayons at work and go to creating a masterpiece. The boss may wonder why you are wasting time, but this will cause you to think in a different way and allow you to come up with more ideas.

Listen to music. You may be inspired by the lyrics. It may make you dance. It may make you silly. It will likely decrease your tension and make writing copy more enjoyable.

Share the knowledge. Bounce ideas off another coworker, friend, or family member. It helps to hear other people's ideas and have their input. They may say something that helps you think in a new direction.

Take random surveys. Bounce ideas off strangers. If you are in the grocery store, try starting a conversation with the woman in front of you. Ask her what she thinks, especially if she is part of your target market. She will be honest; she has no reason to soothe your ego. If she dislikes your idea, ask her what would appeal to her. This is like a free focus group. Sometimes the knowledge gained here is valuable.

Ask a child for help. Children are more likely to give you a huge idea because they have fewer constrictions and vast imaginations. You may have to tone down their ideas, but you may be able to use pieces of what a child has provided.

No One Is Perfect

No matter what your best idea is, someone will dislike it. Do not let this discourage you. You may become attached to copy you have written, but do not be afraid to throw it away. Though you may think your boss or client is being foolish, and perhaps he or she is, this person also may know what is best. If you become too attached to your work, you will not be able to explore new ideas and create new solutions. It will be detrimental for everyone.

If you like your idea, try to sell it to your boss or client. This is where your salesmanship comes in. Explain why you think this idea works to sell the product or service and how it appeals to your target market. If you have facts to back you up, the more inclined your boss or client may be to consider your idea. If he or she still has suggestions, take them into consideration and try to incorporate them into your ad.

Although your feelings may be hurt, you cannot let that get you down. The best thing to do is keep going. It is not the end of the world. Keep writing and giving your best on future advertisements. It takes time to learn how to write effective copy, and it takes time to know your boss and client.

Case Study: Susan Greene

What made you want to become a copywriter?

I decided I wanted to become a writer almost as soon as I learned to read. I loved books, and I always felt a desire to write. Even as a child, I kept journals, wrote short stories, and kept in touch with dozens of pen pals from around the world, most of whom found me via a poem of mine that was published along with my name and address in an Archie comic book.

Even though I did not know what type of writer I wanted to be until my 20s, when I got my first job at an advertising agency, I always knew I would choose a career that was based on my writing abilities.

What was your first assignment? How did you feel about it?

As I mentioned, the first thing I ever had published was a poem I wrote for Archie comics. Each Archie comic book had a small contest area in which they awarded prizes to the top three writers and published their works, often a short story or poem about the Archie characters. A poem I wrote won second place. I received $5. It might as well have been a million; I was so thrilled. The check had a drawing on it of all the Archie characters, and my dad pleaded with me to save the check for posterity. But I really wanted the $5, so I cashed it. Now I wish I had listened to him, since it was the start of my writing career. I think I was about 8 years old.

My actual first copywriting "assignment" was not nearly as much fun. It was a feature article for a New Hampshire business magazine on a local pasta and cheese shop. I think I was paid $100 and given free cheese samples.

What do you know now that you wish you had known when you first started?

Everything. I have learned so much over the years. I guess one of the most important things I now know is that not everyone likes to read as much as I do. So I need to be concise and focus on the key points. Long, rambling paragraphs and excessive amounts of detail will overwhelm and bore the reader.

What is the toughest copywriting challenge that you faced?

Whatever project I am working on at the moment feels like my toughest copywriting challenge. I just have to remind myself that I have somehow managed to get through every previous assignment, and I can get through this one as well.

Case Study: Susan Greene

Some of the harder projects I have worked on were writing about sophisticated high-tech and industrial products. I can remember composing sentences in which I focused on putting the subjects and verbs where I thought they belonged, even though I did not know what the words meant. I wrote on topics like non-ferrous investment castings, ferrofluids, printed circuit boards, and integrating spheres used for spectroscopy. Now I am a pseudo-expert on all kinds of esoteric subjects that hardly anybody knows or cares about.

How does Web copywriting differ from traditional copywriting?

Web copywriting is more conversational and personable than traditional copywriting. It should sound friendly, even casual, like you are talking to a buddy. My goal is often to make sure the reader likes me (or my client) and trusts me (or my client) after reading my copy. I speak to the reader as though we are chatting one-on-one, even using humor when possible. Most of all, I try to make the reader feel my enthusiasm.

When I write for the Web, I make sure to keep my sentences short and simple. My paragraphs are often no more than five lines in length. I use lots of headings, subheads, bullets, and graphic elements. I think big chunks of text on a PC monitor are a turnoff to the reader.

Finally, you cannot talk about Web copywriting without mentioning search engine optimization (SEO). When I write text for a Web site, I think about writing for two audiences: 1) the search engines and 2) the visitor. I make sure to use key words that will attract search engines and then persuasive sentences that will nudge the visitor to take action.

Who are some of the clients you have worked for?

I currently live in Orlando, (Florida,) so, like several copywriters in this city, I have written various promotional materials for theme parks like Walt Disney World and SeaWorld, for hotels and resorts, and for guest services like the I-RIDE Trolleys, which travel through the major tourist areas.

For a long time, I specialized in business-to-business writing, so much of my work was for high-tech and industrial companies. I could tell you the names of the firms, but you likely would not recognize them unless you had worked in those industries.

What copy have you crafted that you loved?

One of the most fun assignments I had was writing about lizards. Yes, lizards. It was an art project for the city of Orlando in which local companies could sponsor seven-

Case Study: Susan Greene

foot statues of lizards designed by area artists — LizArt. The lizards, each created with a different theme, were to be placed in prominent locations all around the city, like in front of city hall and in city parks. I had to write the promotional literature that explained the art project to the sponsors and the artists. Since it was a fun undertaking for the city, I was able to write creative copy and throw in puns. I even had to come up with suggestions for lizard names, like The Lizard of Oz and Lizard Minnelli.

What is your biggest success?

The funny thing is that while I have written many ad campaigns, brochures, and Web sites that have been successful for my clients, I would have to say that my biggest successes — the ones of which I am most proud and that have made me the most money — are copywriting projects I have done for myself. Let me give you two examples:

One is a book that I co-authored called *The Ultimate Job Hunter's Guidebook*. I came up with the idea to create a book that told college students how to prepare their résumé, research companies, and interview successfully. This was back in 1991, and the few books that existed on this topic at the time were complex and boring. I teamed up with a college professor to create an easy-to-use manual for job hunting, complete with hands-on exercises, role-playing scenarios, and practical career advice. We were able to sell the book to Houghton Mifflin, one of the largest academic publishers in the United States. Today, more than 16 years later, that book is in its fifth edition and is considered one of the leading career textbooks used in college courses around the country and the world. Best of all, the royalty checks just keep rolling in.

The second major success would have to be a family business that I helped found in 2004. My father and brother, both real estate brokers, said they had heard of a unique type of real estate product called condo hotels, and they wanted to break into selling these properties. They asked me to help them write a four-page Web site. I easily completed that assignment but then had ideas for expanding it. That four-page Web site soon grew to be 20 pages, then 50, then 100, then 500, and it is now about 800 pages and still growing. Plus we have five other related Web sites. That venture has done well and continues to grow. We have hired sales and support people. We sell properties throughout the world to buyers from all over the world. All marketing is done via the Web. We use no print media. Other than the officers in the company, our employees do not even have business cards. It is truly a global Internet business, and its success is largely due to the Web sites I have built.

Case Study: Susan Greene

The URLs are:

www.CondoHotelCenter.com

www.CentralAmericaSecondHomes.com

www.CondoHotelsDubai.com

www.WorldClassCondoHotels.com

www.CondoHotelsBahamas.com

What is one of the hardest things you find about being a copywriter?

Of course, there is a learning curve whenever you are writing for a new client or about a new product or service. Beyond that, one of the most challenging aspects of being a freelance copywriter is pricing work. Since every project is a custom job, it is hard to work off a set price list. I try to estimate how many hours the project will take and then multiply that number by my hourly rate. As I have become more experienced and confident over the years, I have raised my hourly rate, and I have become more adept in quoting accurately. Nonetheless, I find there is still a bit of guesswork in coming up with a price that is fair compensation for my efforts and also allows my clients to feel they have received good value for their money.

Do you think it is possible to make a decent living as a freelance copywriter?

Yes, but it is hard work. Every project is a custom job. Every client is unique. There is a steep learning curve involved in most things you do. Some days, I find myself thinking it would be so much easier to just sell widgets.

The advice I give freelance copywriters just embarking on their careers is to seek out multiple streams of income. That is, do not just be a writer for others. Find ways to use your writing skills to generate revenue beyond writing for clients. That may mean you use your writing talent to sell affiliate products on auction Web sites like eBay. It may mean you create eBooks or other types of information products that you market online. It could mean going into a partnership with one of your clients in which in lieu of copywriting fees, you get stock in the company or a percentage of sales for your contribution.

In my case, my freelance copywriting revenue is well supplemented by the royalties I get from the textbook I wrote, *The Ultimate Job Hunter's Guidebook*. I also am a

Case Study: Susan Greene

principal in Condo Hotel Center, **www.CondoHotelCenter.com**, an Internet-based real estate company I started with family members.

Can you offer any other advice to freelance copywriters?

Yes, one thing I tell most copywriters trying to launch their careers is to try to be more than "just a writer." If you can also act as a marketing consultant, search engine optimization expert, or find some specialty or copywriting niche that makes you unique and adds value to what you can provide to a client, you will have the ability to 1) differentiate yourself from competitors and 2) charger higher rates (read: less work, more pay).

Susan Greene

Freelance copywriter

407-578-5528

Susan@SusanGreeneCopywriter.com

www.SusanGreeneCopywriter.com

Section 2

How to Write Copy for
Various Online Media

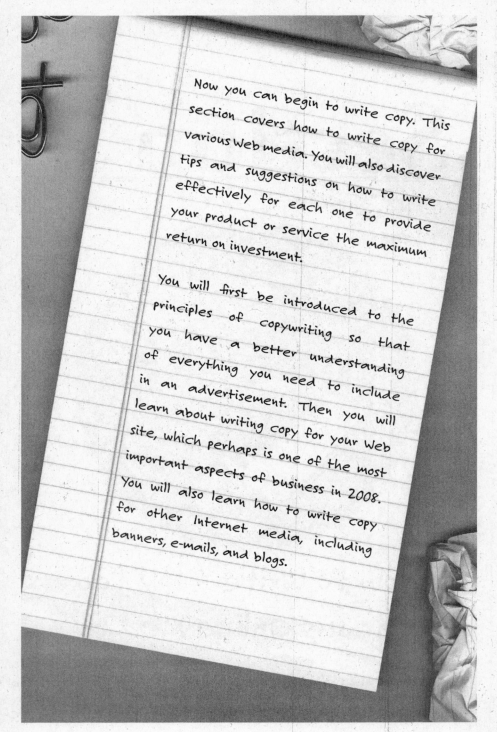

Now you can begin to write copy. This section covers how to write copy for various Web media. You will also discover tips and suggestions on how to write effectively for each one to provide your product or service the maximum return on investment.

You will first be introduced to the principles of copywriting so that you have a better understanding of everything you need to include in an advertisement. Then you will learn about writing copy for your Web site, which perhaps is one of the most important aspects of business in 2008. You will also learn how to write copy for other Internet media, including banners, e-mails, and blogs.

Extra, Extra
Read All About It

"I glance at the headlines just to kind of get a flavor for what is moving. I rarely read the stories and get briefed by people who are reading the news themselves."
President George W. Bush

An advertisement contains many elements. These elements work together to create an effective advertisement. This chapter focuses on the headline, which is often the first thing a reader sees and reads on an advertisement. The following chapters are dedicated to other advertising elements.

There are three important things to remember when writing a headline:

1.   It is important to grab your reader's attention.

2.   The headline, like other advertising elements, is designed to make the consumer read the first line of copy.

3.   Headlines, especially those used on the Web, should be conversational.

Headline

This is what the reader sees first. It needs to draw the reader into the advertisement and make him or her want to read more. There are a few rules to writing good headlines.

Headlines should be written in an active voice. This is a rule that carries through in all writing and is one that should rarely be broken. It again holds through in writing copy, especially since you are writing to drive a sale. Make the subject of the sentence the consumer if possible, or use "you."

> **Bad headline:** The guacamole most preferred by consumers was Guac-n-Rock Guacamole

> **Good headline:** Consumers most prefer Guac-n-Rock Guacamole

The first example is too wordy. Guacamole is the subject of the sentence, when the point of the sentence relates to consumers.

Headlines should use present tense and have a strong verb.

There is no sense in saying things in past tense when you want the consumer to act now. Using past tense makes consumers think that what you are selling has already occurred. You need them to believe it is occurring now. Use a strong verb to help add excitement to your headline.

Bad headline: Guac-n-Rock Guacamole was tasty

Good headline: Guac-n-Rock Guacamole tastes great

The first example implies that the guacamole was once tasty but perhaps it is not now. The second example says that the guacamole is still tasty. It also uses a strong, active verb, rather than using a form of the verb "to be."

A headline should be specific. Since it is the first line of copy, and likely the first part of the advertisement a consumer reads, it should list specifics instead of being vague.

Bad headline: Guacamole company produces new flavor

Good headline: Guac-n-Rock Guacamole introduces new, spicy flavor

The first headline does not say which company or what flavor. A consumer would not pay any attention to it, and if he or she happened to read the headline, the consumer would not know anything about it or why it should interest him or her. The second example brands the guacamole and mentions there is a new, spicy flavor. Consumers who like spicy foods would be more inclined to read more.

A headline should use short, punchy words. Not everyone will expand his or her vocabulary to try and decipher your headline. Thus, it is easier to use words that the consumer already understands.

Bad headline: Guac-n-Rock Guacamole affirms the high caliber of its guacamole products

Good headline: Guac-n-Rock Guacamole uses real Hass avocados in its guacamole

The first headline leaves a reader wondering what is trying to be said. Why would a company be affirming high caliber of something? It is not good to leave a reader confused for any reason.

There are no specific word criteria for the headline. It can be one word or it can be ten. However, headlines should not be wordy and should get straight to the point.

Bad headline: Delicious Guac-n-Rock Guacamole delivers a new and improved product line that includes variations of spicy guacamoles

Good headline: Guac-n-Rock Guacamole introduces new, spicy guacamole flavor

The first example can lose the reader. He or she may have no idea what you are saying. The second example is succinct and says the same thing.

A headline should be inventive. When you are trying to get the attention of a reader, you have to be creative and make your headline pop.

Bad headline: Guacamole tastes good

Good headline: Have a fiesta in your mouth

The first example is ambiguous. What does "good" mean to someone? Different people have different meanings. You need to let your consumers experience what "good" means so that they know what to expect when using your product. The second example helps the consumer experience the taste of Rock-n-Guac Guacamole by letting them know that the guacamole is like a party in their mouth, implying that the guacamole is not only "good," but it is fun as well.

Other Extras

Do not use exclamation points in your headlines. These make it seem like your words need extra emphasis, when your phrase should speak for itself without any extra help. Exclamation points make your headlines look contrived and forced rather than appearing to be conversational and factual.

When possible, use quotations in your headlines. Copywriter and marketer Ted Nicholas conducted a test to discover which copy elements boost response rates. He determined that an ad headline draws 28 percent more attention when framed in quotation marks. The quotation marks make the advertisement appear more important.

Primary Headline Functions

A headline provides four primary functions for the reader:

- ✐ Gets the reader's attention

- ✐ Defines the audience

- Delivers a message

- Directs the reader to the body copy

There are several ways to get a reader's attention through a headline. One way to gain attention is to promise the reader something. If you can legitimately use the word free, then do so in the headline. The word "free" is known to grab readers' attention because they want to know what is free.

Bright Idea

Make sure that you do not use the word "free" excessively. Search engines will think your page is spam.

However, free is not always an option, so using other attention-grabbing words and phrases, such as the following, may help gain attention.

- Discover

- New

- Introducing

- How to...

- Four easy steps to...

- Reduce

- Easy

- Learn

Pulling from the earlier example of Guac-n-Rock Guacamole, an attention-getting headline may be: "Discover a new way to prevent cancer" (a study by The Ohio State University discovered that avocados may help prevent oral cancer).

When you define the audience, you narrow down whom the advertisement is directed toward. For example, an advertisement for Guac-n-Rock Guacamole might read, "Hey, Teenagers, add some flavor to your food." This headline gears the advertisement toward teenagers, and if someone is not a teenager, he or she is likely to stop reading the advertisement.

Bright Idea

Your headline is one of the most important pieces of copy that you can write.

Many readers read only the headline and skip the rest of the advertisement. Thus, it is a good idea to have a complete idea contained in your headline. An example may be, "Rock-n-Guac Guacamole may help prevent oral cancer." This is similar to the attention-getting example, except it brands the headline and tells what kind of cancer may help be prevented. The reader does not have to read more to understand the advertisement.

Headline Categories

Robert W. Bly lists eight different headline categories in his book *The Copywriter's Handbook*. A headline often falls into one of these categories:

   Direct headlines

- Indirect headlines

- News headlines

- How-to headlines

- Question headlines

- Command headlines

- Reason why headlines

- Testimonial headlines

Direct Headlines

Direct headlines get straight to the point of what you want the advertisement to say and do. These are often found in newspapers with sales headlines. An example might be, "Guac-n-Rock Guacamole 50 Percent Off — This Week Only."

Indirect Headlines

Indirect headlines do not get straight to the point. The indirect headline could have a double meaning, and often a reader may have to read the body copy to understand what the headline is saying. These headlines are supposed to pique a reader's curiosity; however, they require more thought from the reader and may require more knowledge to be able to fully comprehend. This could turn potential consumers away from the advertisement. An example may be, "Turn your mouth green."

News Headlines

News headlines deliver news about your product. If you have a new product, this headline may work best for you. Assume that Guac-n-Rock Guacamole is a new brand on the market. The news headline may be the best headline to use for your Web site. This is because Web copy needs to be written conversationally and appear more as an editorial than as an advertisement. A news headline may read, "Introducing a new pre-made guacamole that contains actual avocados."

How-to Headlines

How-to headlines begin with the words "how to" and give the reader a clue on how to do something, with the directions being stated in the body copy. An example for Guac-n-Rock Guacamole would be, "How to reduce your cholesterol while eating flavorful foods."

Question Headlines

Question headlines ask questions that a reader would like to see answered. These headlines should be directed at the reader's self-interest and curiosity. They should be questions that readers want to know the answer to and questions readers ask in their everyday lives. An example may be, "Would you like to reduce your cholesterol while eating flavorful foods?"

Command Headlines

Command headlines tell readers what to do. They should contain a strong verb that engages the reader and makes him or her want to act. An example would be, "Eat more vegetables."

Reason Why Headlines

Reason why headlines give reasons why using a product or service is beneficial. The body copy then details the reasons in order. An example might be, "Eight Ways Avocados Make You Healthy" or "Five Steps to Preparing the Perfect Party."

Testimonial Headlines

Testimonial headlines contain quotes by other people. They should be written as conversationally as possible, as if spoken by the customer. This technique is used often in dieting products or sweepstakes. An example may be, "Guac-n-Rock Guacamole Helped Save My Snack Food, and It Can Help Save Yours, Too."

Choosing a Headline

Sometimes, you write several headlines and find one you like; sometimes, you write 100 and do not like any of them. Do not become so entangled in your work that you dislike a headline because you do not find it clever or exciting. As an advertiser, your definition of clever and exciting may be different from the consumer's.

Also, if you narrow it down to two headlines, one that you think is clever and exciting but that you are not sure appeals to the consumer, and one that will appeal to the consumer but is dry, pick the latter. You may not win any awards, but you will sell the product. This goes back to the main point of writing copy being to sell the product.

Since your headline will often direct the artwork to be included (or the artwork will direct the headline), you need to make sure the headline is effective and understandable. Run your ideas by as many people as possible and ask for suggestions. You may be on the verge of something great, but someone else may provide a valuable suggestion that could cause you to tweak your advertisement into something special.

Case Study: Debra Jason

What made you want to become a copywriter?

The short story: In 1988, I took a direct-response writing workshop with veteran Milt Pierce at New York University (NYU). Each time I submitted a "homework assignment," he would rave about my skills and read my project aloud to the class. Then he referred me to the late Eugene Schwartz (another direct-mail veteran). With each of them behind me, I developed my skills and gained the confidence I needed to go out on my own as a copywriter.

The longer story: I had been working with a catalog company in Colorado, managing the catalog from start to finish (from 1983 to 1987). After a few years, I decided I wanted to something less administrative and more creative. I asked my boss if I could write, and she said "yes." So, I started out writing catalog product copy. Then, I moved to New York, where I took Milt's workshop while working at Grey Direct in 1988. I took a job as a traffic manager just to get in the door until they had an opening for a copywriter. They kept saying, "in six months, in six months." Rather than wait, I returned to Colorado and started my freelance business, The Write Direction. That was in 1989.

What was your first assignment? How did you feel about it?

My first paid assignment was working on a direct-mail letter for Eugene Schwartz. He promoted self-help books. It required reading the book first, taking notes, developing a lengthy "vocabulary" that was then entered in the computer (covering pages and pages of information), and then referring to that "vocabulary" to gather strong benefits and write long direct-mail letters. It was challenging, but Gene taught me what I needed to know.

How does Web copywriting differ from traditional copywriting?

When writing Web site content, I focus on key word phrases — those phrases viewers might be using to search for a site on a search engine. It is important to repeat those key words in specific places on the Web page, but there is a limit

Case Study: Debra Jason

on how often to repeat them (you do not want the search engine to think you are "spamming" it). When writing a brochure (traditional copywriting), I avoid using the same phrases repeatedly, as it just does not read well.

Who are some of the clients you have worked for?

Intellidyn Corporation, The Hamilton Collection, Tec de Monterrey: Study in Mexico, Cahners Publishing, HealthSmart Vitamins, Fran Tarkenton Small Business NETwork, and more. A partial client list is online at **www.writedirection. com/clients.htm**. You can find client testimonials at **www.writedirection.com/ testmonials.htm**.

What are the best tips you have for successful Web copywriting?

Gain readers' attention, hold their interest, create desire, and do not forget a call to action. Even if you have a button on your Web site that says "order here" or "become a member," the content should ask for a call to action as well.

I write benefit-oriented copy first, thinking about what "buttons" I can push so that while he or she is reading, the prospect thinks, "Yes, that is me. Yes, I need that," and so on. Then, once the buttons are pushed, I can offer them solutions or answers that make them want to act and take advantage of the offer, buy the product or service, pick up the phone, visit the Web site, and so on.

For more details on tips, read my "How-To Report "on my Web site **www. writedirection.com/how-to.htm** (REPORT #300B).

Do you feel it is more important in copywriting to be creative or a salesperson?

It depends on what your client wants. With direct marketing, the goal is to sell and get results. However, you are always being creative — that is why people hire you. They want someone who is creative and has the skills to combine that creativity with the know-how of selling a product or service.

Some clients do not want "hard sell." For instance, they want to use their Web site not to find new clients but to direct existing prospects to the site so that prospects may gather information easily about why they may or may not want to do business with that company. I am working on a Web site like that now. The client is not concerned about people searching for and finding his site online. He is using it as a vehicle to make it easier for prospects (which he will send to the site) to get to know his company better.

What part of the Web do you find it easiest and hardest to write for (Web sites, banner ads, or e-mail) and why?

Case Study: Debra Jason

I have done only Web pages and e-mail campaigns. The Web pages are easier. The e-mails are often more challenging, because there is much to say and not much space to do it in, so you have to fine-tune the content. In some cases, where recipients have opted-in to hear from you, the message can be longer, but the goal is often to get them to click through to the Web site for more information.

How do you succeed in writing Web copy?

I have been fortunate in that for many clients, I have written content and boosted their positioning in search engines. With search engines changing their algorithms constantly and with pay-per-click competition, this is getting harder to achieve.

Other success tips: Persistence, patience, doing research, listening to my clients (getting good direction on what they "truly" want is vital). I provide each client with a strategy questionnaire to complete before we begin. It helps them gather their thoughts. And it provides me with valuable information to use as a starting point.

The Write Direction

P.O. Box 608

Hanalei, HI 96714

808-826-1846

www.writedirection.com

The Other Copy Elements

"There are so many different kinds of writing and so many ways to work that the only rule is this: Do what works. Almost everything has been tried and found to succeed for somebody."
Sophy Burnham

After you have written the headline that has drawn the attention of the reader, other elements can be used in the advertisement to sustain the reader's attention.

Subheadline

The subheadline further explains the headline. It helps the reader gain more interest in the advertisement, because it starts to explain what the advertisement is about. It often explains the core benefits of the product or service and encourages a reader to continue reading the body copy to understand the real value of what your business is offering.

The subhead is smaller than the headline and is often located below the headline. One subhead or multiple ones can be used in the advertisement.

Some copywriters do not like subheads and would rather explain the headline in the first sentence of the body copy. There is no right or wrong answer on whether to have a subheadline; rather, it is the copywriter's personal preference. However, when the average reader just skims advertisements in the first place, it makes sense to use a subheadline; it stands out and is easier for the reader to pick up the beneficial pieces of information. Otherwise, the reader may skip the body copy and never know the true benefit of your product or service.

Photo or Illustration

Artwork is used to draw a reader into the advertisement and make him or her want to read the copy. A large picture or illustration is like a headline in the sense that it is one of the first things to grab a reader's attention and pull him or her into the advertisement.

If you are using a large photo or illustration, it should be attention-grabbing and not just a boring snapshot of your product. Unless your product is new and exciting or does something extraordinary, a consumer will not stop and read the advertisement.

The dominant photo or illustration, if you choose to have one, should be something that ties into the headline. These two elements of the advertisement should be cohesive and work together to grab the consumer's attention and keep him or her reading.

Within the body copy of the advertisement, you can place other pictures. These can be photos of the product or illustrations on how the product works. These will be working with the body copy and need to work into the flow of the advertisement.

Do not place a photo or illustration for no reason. Make sure it has a purpose and needs to be there. The consumer will likely see the photograph or illustration, so make sure it is something worth looking at.

The photo should be cropped properly to fully illustrate the part that the consumer needs to be looking at. The photograph should also be in focus and not grainy or pixilated.

Photo Caption

If you have a photograph or illustration of your product, it may be necessary to have a caption describing or explaining it.

The caption should explain the content of your photo or illustration in detail. Since this text is offset from the body copy and other elements of the advertisement, the consumer may be drawn to read it because it is distinguishable.

Captions are especially important if you are showing an illustration of your product. These help explain what is going on and enable the consumer to have a clear understanding. Imagine what it would be like to read the owner's manual on how to put together a bicycle without pictures and captions to show what is going on. Use these captions to help the reader.

Paragraph Headings

Paragraph headings are used to break up your body copy, if necessary. They help give the reader a break from the monotonous mountain of words that you, as a copywriter, have laid out, and they make it easier to digest what has been said.

Paragraph headings also allow the consumer more freedom to skip around the advertisement and read what he or she wants to read. Headings may also engage a consumer so much that he or she decides to read a particular section.

These headings are often bold and a little larger than the rest of the body copy, which allows the consumer to see them more clearly.

Body Copy

The body copy is the meat and potatoes of the advertisement. This is where you lay out everything that you want the consumer to know about the product and sell it.

The other elements listed have been used to get the consumer so interested in the product or service that he or she needs to read the first line of the body copy. Now, the first line of the body copy must get the consumer to read the second line. Then the second line must get the consumer to read the third line of body copy, and so on to the end of the advertisement.

The body copy should be structured to flow easily. It should move flawlessly from one word to the next, one paragraph to the next, and cause the reader to keep reading.

There are certain aesthetics to keep in mind when writing body copy:

It should be easy to read. Pick a legible font, preferably one of the standard fonts on everyone's computer, such as Arial or Times New Roman (we will discuss typography in greater detail in a later chapter).

Make sure the font is large enough to see. This size will vary, but for body copy, a good rule of thumb is to never make it less than 10 points, and it should never be a greater size than the paragraph head, subheadline, or headline. Do not make it more than 14 points.

Make sure there is enough space between your sentences. Your sentences should not be on top of each other.

Make sure there is enough space between your words. You do not want your words to blend together. If you are using a design program such as InDesign, you can adjust the tracking between your words. The best advice is to not adjust it, unless you feel your sentences are smashed together, and then you may want to increase the tracking. However, it is often noticeable when you increase or decrease tracking, so be cautious when using this tool.

Make sure that all text easily wraps around pictures. Also, you want to make sure that there is enough text above or below a picture that the consumer knows to read it. In other words, do not put a single sentence above or below a picture. A consumer may skip over it, and that sentence could be important to the advertisement.

Now that you have some idea of the standard design principles of typography, you can focus on the more important task at hand — selling your product or service.

Engage the consumer in every word of your type. Use emotional words that appeal to the reader rather than complex words that he or she may not easily understand. Do not assume that consumers will skip over the body copy. Not all of them will. Make sure that once you have the consumer read the first sentence, you keep his or her attention until you make the sale at the end of the body copy.

Logo

Company logos are often displayed in the lower-right corner of an advertisement. A consumer's eye often scans the advertisement in the form of a letter "z," making the ending space the lower-right corner. By placing your logo here, the company logo will be the last thing the reader sees before moving past the advertisement. This allows for more brand recognition and greater remembrance of the company.

If a logo is not placed in the lower-right corner, it should be placed somewhere on the page. Most companies choose to place their logo at the bottom of the page somewhere, be it the lower-left corner or the middle of the page toward the bottom. It is important that the consumer knows who the business is so that he or she can easily recall it at a later time.

Price

Sometimes advertisers choose to display the price of their product in the advertisement. This is often done when there is a sale going on for the product. The price gets the reader's attention. It may not be the price, as in $19.95. Instead, it may be something like, "Buy one, get one free."

Car companies frequently use price in their advertisements. When you see a car advertisement, it often says, "Starting at $_____." The price gives the reader the knowledge of how much the product costs and whether he or she can afford that price.

This is another method that an advertiser can use to segment readers. For example, if you sell Porsche vehicles and you list your price as $80,999, someone making $25,000 a year is likely not in the market for your product. However, that price tag may appeal to someone who earns $250,000 a year. Displaying the price also helps the advertiser from having the customer who earns only $25,000 a year try to purchase the $80,999 vehicle.

This method of segmenting your target audience by displaying price is often done on higher-end products, such as cars, for these reasons. By contrast, you likely would not find an advertisement for soda displaying its price.

Response Device

A response device gives the consumer a way to contact the advertiser. Many advertisers list their Web site's Uniform Resource Locator (URL) in all forms of their advertisements. Doing this allows a consumer to log on to the Web site for more information, and there is often a way to contact the company from the Web site (often found under a "Contact Us" link).

Another popular response device is listing the company's phone number. This allows the consumer a direct way to contact the company. The phone number is listed for businesses that can provide you with direct service over the phone. You can see this type of contact used in commercials for insurance companies, but you would not see it used in a commercial for Wal-Mart.

Direct-response devices can also be something as simple as a coupon. When you use the coupon, it lets the business know you saw or heard the advertisement and that you liked the product or service enough to give it a try. Coupons are good response devices because they encourage trial usage and allow consumers to spend less money than they might to see if they like a new product. If the product is good, they are likely to continue using it.

Bright Idea

Include a response device in your advertising to help drive your sales.

Another response device is an order form. This allows the consumer to fill out a form and send it to the company — for whatever reason. When the company receives the order form that has been taken from the advertisement, they know the advertisement is effective. It is also able to collect the consumer's contact information and can use it in a later effort to contact consumers for future sales or promotions it may have. Staying connected with the consumer gives the company an opportunity to make future sales.

A Call to Action

Displaying a "call to action" button or link is especially important in Web advertising. This is where the consumer commits to purchasing your product or service. A good example of a call to action that most everyone is familiar with are those displayed on infomercials. They scatter about call to actions and display their phone number. Often, they will say things like, "Call within the next 15 minutes and receive free shipping" or some other offer.

On your Web site, you can do the same thing. You can say, "From June 1 to June 15, you will receive free shipping with your order" or "From June 1 to June 15, you will receive an upgrade." You can always change the dates after they expire. However, setting a limitation for your offer will make consumers act faster because they have the perception of getting a deal.

A good example of a Web site that has a call to action is **www. tryabrocket.com/?cid=475601**. Here, you will find an "order now" button at the top which will direct you to the bottom of the page. Of course, if you read through the entire page, you will also be presented with the call to action button at the bottom of the page, where you can fill out your checkout information.

Always provide a link to where consumers can purchase your product. This may only be a link in your advertisements, or it may be checkout information on your Web site.

The Layout

The last element we will examine is the layout of the advertisement. Though this is not a true element unto itself, it is important to analyze the look and feel of the advertisement as a whole.

When you look at the advertisement, ask yourself the following questions:

- Is it cohesive?

- Is it aesthetically pleasing?

- Is it attention-grabbing?

- Does it go together?

- Is it easily readable?

- Would I stop and read this?

- Would my target market stop and read this?

If you answered no to any of these questions, it does not necessarily mean your advertisement is bad, but it does mean you should go back over it and possibly reconsider it before publishing it.

Now, consider the following questions:

- Does anything stand out or look awkward?

- Is there too much blank space?

- Is it too crowded?

- Is it overwhelming?

If you answered yes to any of these questions, again, this does not necessarily mean your advertisement is bad. Take the time to look over it. Let someone else look over it and see what he or she thinks. Test it on members of your target audience before launching the campaign and see what they have to say — their opinion is the one that truly matters.

Bright Idea

Your advertisement campaign needs to have a cohesive synergy.

Some advertisements contain more body copy than others. The amount depends on the size of the advertisement and the recognition of the brand/business name. Extensive body copy may not be necessary for some clients, whereas it may be vital for others.

If you are starting a small business or have just created a new product, leaving out body copy would be a big mistake, unless there is no way to avoid it because of space limitations. The body copy is where you can flesh out an idea and give complete details about your product or service. If your consumers are unfamiliar with your product, it is especially important to use body copy. If, for some reason, you find that you cannot incorporate body copy, be sure to direct the consumer to a place (perhaps your Web site) where he or she can find more information.

An Overview of Commercials

Though this book is about writing copy for the Web, it should be noted that not all these elements apply in true form to commercials (advertisements that are broadcast). Since the Web is moving increasingly to a broadcast base that allows consumers to hear audio and watch video, it is important to address a few differences between print and broadcast elements.

Radio, TV, and Internet commercials still use the previous elements, with a few differences.

You have only the first couple of seconds to gain the consumer's attention in a commercial. Thus, the first few words and visuals are vital. These words are equivalent to a headline, because they capture the viewer's/listener's attention. If you lose the consumer in the first few seconds, he or she will not pay attention to the rest of the commercial, so it is important to hook the consumer in the beginning.

The next few seconds are roughly comparable to subheadlines because this clarifies what you did to catch the consumer's attention in the first place. These sentences should blend into the relevant body copy as well.

Body copy for a commercial is shorter than in a print advertisement. This is because you have less time to say what you want. Commercials last anywhere between 15 and 60 seconds, and you realize quickly that time is of the essence. A video that you place on your Web site could be different in the time that you have allowed because it is on the company site and does not cost money for each airing. Still, you need to catch and keep the consumer's attention.

Visuals have a major impact in commercials. They guide a consumer through the commercial and illustrate the words being spoken. There may not be any captions for these visuals; however, the spoken copy may be a guide to what these visuals represent.

Response devices are as important in commercials as they are in print advertisements. They serve the exact same purpose and help consumers form connections with businesses.

Summary

No advertising element is more important than any other. What attracts you to read an advertisement may be different from what attracts your best friend. You may be a visual person and look straight to those details, whereas your friend may see the headline and want to read more based on that. This is why all these elements are designed to get the consumer to read the first line of copy.

The body copy is where the sell is made. It contains all the vital information that consumers need to know. It should be easy to read and understand, keep your attention, and flow seamlessly.

There should always be a logo, or business or brand recognition, somewhere in the advertisement. This helps the consumer retain the brand information for a later purchase. Also, give the consumer a response device so that he or she can easily contact the business for more information.

Case Study: Kristen Fischer

What made you want to become a copywriter?

I fell into copywriting. After working as a journalist and in the technical communications arena, I realized I could make more money writing for businesses. I liked that I'd get to explore all industries. I worked my way up doing projects on the side for about two years and then I took a part-time editing job and used the days to further build my business and abilities. I've been solo for about three years now.

What was your first assignment? How did you feel about it?

As a copywriter I had to write a brochure about a senior health facility. I really enjoyed it because I learned how copywriting differed from journalism, and also found out how print and Web writing differed.

What do you know now that you wish you had known when you first started?

I wish I knew that it was okay to doubt myself and my abilities, and that I'd need to reach out for help. I experienced a lot of self-doubt and ultimately wound up publishing my first book, Creatively Self-Employed: How Writers and Artists Deal with Career Ups and Downs out of it. It was great compiling the book because I really connected with people and became friends with a lot of creatives who understood self-employment from the experience.

What is the toughest copywriting challenge that you faced?

Sometimes just the topic of something can put me off. I've had to write about tumor testing, waste removal, urology, and now I'm doing a huge SEO project for an industrial waste company. When I first hear about the projects they don't sound appealing, so it can be tough to get motivated. But I'm not a procrastinator, I'm pretty great about getting things done—and I never miss a deadline.

How does Web copywriting differ from traditional copywriting?

This isn't really a matter of opinion—more so fact. Web is more succinct and easier on the eye.

Who are some of the clients that you have worked for?

Trane, MediaPost, Dow Jones. I work for various agencies and have gotten large clients through them as well.

Case Study: Kristen Fischer

What is your biggest success? What copy have you crafted that you really loved?

I recently did a brochure for a woman who provides emotional coverage. Similar to how the life insurance works, her business allows people to leave behind letters to the ones they loved. When I first heard about it, I thought it would be a total downer to write. But the client was great and I really felt like I was helping people by enabling them to understand why this was so important. Plus there aren't other companies like that right now, so it was sort of groundbreaking. The site is http://copelandclosure.com/ if you want to see more.

What are the best tips you have for successful Web copywriting?

First, I think you have to have some natural writing ability. Not just the skill to write, but to write well. You have to be a natural writer, editor and proofreader. For me, I was always stronger in writing but never thought to make a career out of it. I always knew I wanted to write a book but never realized that I could make a living with words. I had a strong grammar background and picked up expertise in styles—especially AP—along the way. So you can't just write, you have to be a good writer.

For Web copywriting, you need to study the craft and learn about the trends in web writing. It's not the same as anything else. Getting in with an SEO agency has helped me tremendously.

Do you feel that it is more important in copywriting to be creative or a salesman?

Salesman. Absolutely. If you're not a natural writer you won't enter copywriting, most likely. If you are, you'll have to rely on more than your talent to stay in business—especially if you go the self-employed route. Not a lot of creatives realize they need to be professional and get involved in things like marketing, accounting and business development. I'm lucky to have some of these skills—except accounting—that come innately for me. For those I don't (have I mentioned I detest numbers?) I hire an accountant.

What part of the Web do you find it easiest and hardest to write for (Web sites, banner ads, e-mail, etc.) and why?

I specialize mostly in Web sites, so I'd have to say simple site content. My experience in journalism helped me learn extensively about headlines, so I can pretty much write for any form.

How do you succeed in writing Web copy?

Case Study: Kristen Fischer

I continually market myself more than I actually write, sometimes. I have built an impressive portfolio of links and use that to leverage my marketing. Plus, I don't just rely on job openings for work.

What makes the Internet a great media for advertising?

It's not only convenient, but it is the premier media now. Companies must embrace this! For me as a copywriter, having a Web site has been an indispensable resource. I'm also using the Net to promote my newest book, Ramen Noodles, Rent and Resumes: An After-College Guide to Life. I'm pulling together my copywriting background and my experience with public relations to market the book and having great success!

Kristen Fischer

www.kristenfischer.com

Point Pleasant, NJ

Your Web Site

*"They say a year in the Internet business is like a dog year,
equivalent to seven years in a regular person's life.
In other words, it is evolving fast and faster."*
Vinton Cerf

Most advertisements these days direct consumers to the company's Web site. If it is an online advertisement, it may not have much body copy, if any, because if the consumer clicks on the advertisement, it will route him or her back to the company's Web site, where the sell should be made. Otherwise, many print advertisements and TV commercials contain the company's URL. This again directs the consumer to the company's Web site to learn more information. Nonetheless, with every advertisement pointing toward your Web site, it is a pivotal hub in selling your product.

Your Web site can have a variety of purposes, and its shape and content depend on why you need the Web site to begin with. If you are using your Web site as the sole portal to sell your product, it will look different than if you are using your Web site to provide consumers more information about a product, which will look different than if you have a brick-and-mortar store and sell your products online. This will still look different than if you are using your Web site to support more name recognition.

Bright Idea

Make sure that your Web site connects with your consumers.

The Fun Web Site

Many well-known companies have fun Web sites, where they promote their name and do little else. An example of this type of Web site is the one for Burger King. Burger King would have a difficult time selling hamburgers and fries through its Web site, so that is not their main purpose for having one. These fun Web sites pull out all the bells and whistles for the purpose of entertaining their consumers.

Burger King has been known for having a creative Web site. The company has multiple extensions of its **www.burgerking.com** site, providing creative activities to entertain its consumers. One such site is the subservient chicken site, which lets consumers type actions they want the chicken to do (**www.subservientchicken. com**). The company has also created an angry gram, which allows consumers to send people a rude message delivered by an angry Whopper hamburger (**www.angry-gram.com**). The point of these sites is to give consumers something fun to do while pushing the Burger King name.

Burger King knows its target consumers in detail and takes high efforts to appeal to them. These offbeat efforts would not appeal to 80-year-old women, but they do appeal to 18-year-old boys.

The Informative Web Site

This approach is used all the time with medications. These Web sites provide useful information that is too lengthy to be contained in advertisements, but these companies are directed by law to provide this information. These companies cannot sell their products online because the purchase of these products requires a doctor's approval. Rather, they use their Web sites to provide information to their consumers.

Take, for example, Paxil's Web site (**www.paxilcr.com**). The home page is dedicated to explaining what the medication does. It provides links to other information about depression and anxiety orders. It provides tests so that you can make a self-diagnosis. It gives you information about what you can do for yourself. Then it tells you to ask your doctor about getting a prescription for the medication.

The Web site is simple and easy to navigate. It provides information you would want to know about the medication and about the conditions associated with it. It then tells you where to obtain the medication.

Medication Web sites employ strong copywriting skills to keep the reader's attention so he or she reads more about the product. Though they do not ask for the sale on their Web site (only because they cannot legally), these companies hope to drive the consumer to seek their doctor's prescription and then purchase the product.

The Brick-and-Mortar Store + Selling Web Site

These Web sites are common for large retail stores, such as Wal-Mart or JCPenney's. They provide you with an online retail store that you can browse and shop at without having to go to the physical store. They do not have to sell you on the products or the company because you already know what they are. They do, however, contain brief descriptions about products, such as sheet thread count or materials used.

Consumers can choose whether to purchase a product online or go to the physical store and purchase the product. They can view the sales advertisements online and see if there is anything at the store on sale they might want to purchase. These Web sites do not provide much detail about the products or company, because it is assumed knowledge. The sole purpose of the Web site is not to inform, nor is it to sell, but rather, it is an extension of the store created for consumers who would rather shop from home.

These Web sites are often plain. They do not use fancy graphics, but rather, they have a picture of the product and the option for a consumer to add the item to a shopping cart. There is no real copywriting involved on these sites, except to give a brief description of the product.

The Sole Selling Web Site

The purpose of the sole selling Web site is to sell a product. Often, this product is not sold in stores or it has a limited distribution. The key is to grab the reader's attention and hook him or her into reading on until the point of introducing the sale.

A good example is **www.webcopywritinguniversity.com**. This is a course provided by Web copywriter Maria Veloso. She starts off the Web page by hooking the reader's attention, and then she gives reasons why you should take her course and testimonials from people who have taken the course. She keeps your attention throughout her lengthy copy and then asks for your sale by clicking a link and typing your information.

Not all Web sites are crafted as successfully as Maria's. The Web site **www.theultimatedietformula.com**, which is a site that sells a weight-loss drug, does not do as good a job at catching the reader's interest and pulling him or her into the sale. However, it still applies the same principles as Veloso's site by trying to get the reader to read the copy and then asking for the sale at the bottom.

These sites are most effective without fancy graphics, which are often hard for many consumers to load on their computers. The words are what do the selling, not the graphics.

The next chapter will go into more detail about how to craft Web copy for this type of Web site.

Case Study: Lisa J. Lehr

www.justrightcopy.com

lisa.justrightcopy@gmail.com

What made you want to become a copywriter?

I have always loved to write. My writing career has taken me through a number of genres, from freelance article writing to editing to ghostwriting to teaching people how to write their autobiographies.

I also have a completed novel manuscript. Copywriting is one of the most satisfying forms of writing because the benefit to the client is so obvious and immediate. Even those clients who are a little skeptical at first, as soon as they see that working with a professional copywriter does make money for them, they are often eager for more.

What do you know now that you wish you had known when you first started?

I wish I had known that you have never truly "arrived" as a copywriter. It is a continuous learning experience. The more you learn, the more you want to learn and improve your skills. What I wrote last year is not as good as what I write now; what I write now is not as good as what I will write next year. That is why copywriters' fees tend to go up so sharply in the first few years — their work gets exponentially better in a short time.

What is the toughest copywriting challenge you faced?

I would not say this was a single experience but more of a recurring theme. It is the client or potential client who needs convincing that professional copywriting is worth paying for. So many people are shocked at the fee quoted and say (in a huff, often) that they are going to do it themselves. Then they wonder why their latest promotion did no better than the last one. Sometimes they can be educated… sometimes they cannot.

How does Web copywriting differ from traditional copywriting?

Ultimately, good copywriting is good copywriting, although there are differences between online and offline copy. Online, it is harder to hold the reader's interest. They have one hand on the mouse, ready to click away at the first twinge of boredom. Navigation has to be straightforward. Layout and design are important, because people tend to expect a certain look and feel. In addition, while people sometimes set a letter aside to respond to later, once they have left your Web page, they may be gone for good.

Case Study: Lisa J. Lehr

What are the best tips you have for successful Web copywriting?

I would say study it from two angles: as a copywriter and as an Internet user. In the former role, learn from the experts and follow their advice. In the latter role, be aware of your own Internet user behavior. What made you decide to buy from this Web site and not that one? What held your attention? What bored, frustrated, or insulted you? There is a good chance that whatever your experiences are, other Internet users react the same way.

Do you feel it is more important in copywriting to be creative or a salesperson?

It is more important to be a salesperson. Creativity and cleverness are mainly for entertainment and for winning awards (and often only the people competing for the awards even know who won them). Think of all the clever print ads, radio jingles, and billboards you have been exposed to. You may get a smile out of them, but do you hurry to buy the product or service? Creativity is overrated. Scientific testing has proved that good salesmanship is what sells.

How do you succeed in writing Web copy?

The most important thing is knowing how to write sales copy. That said, there are differences between online and offline writing. People's attention spans are shorter on the Internet, because it is harder to read the screen. So you have to make it an easy and pleasant experience for them. There is also a predictable way in which a viewer's eyes travel across the screen, so the words that appear on certain parts of the page carry more weight. You have to know how to combine good copywriting with Internet user behavior.

What makes the Internet a great media for advertising?

The big thing is that almost everyone uses the Internet. It is also a great equalizer. With brick-and-mortar businesses, it is all about size, location, certain things you do not necessarily have control over. With the Internet, the underdog can compete with a big, established competitor. If an entrepreneur understands the power of an effective Internet marketing campaign, he or she is in a good position to compete in the marketplace.

Which companies do you feel do best by advertising on the Internet?

All companies need to advertise on the Internet. These days, most people use the Internet for shopping, research and comparison, locations and hours of local businesses, or all of these. So it does not matter if you are local, national, or international — you need to have an Internet presence. If you do not, you are

Case Study: Lisa J. Lehr

putting yourself at a serious disadvantage. But, based on the previous question, small and unknown companies often have the most to gain by advertising on the Internet.

Lisa J. Lehr is a freelance copywriter specializing in direct response and marketing collateral, with a special interest in the health, pets, specialty foods, and inspirational/motivational/self-help niches. She has a degree in biology; has worked in a variety of fields, including pharmaceuticals and teaching; and has volunteered for many causes, including special-needs children and literacy. When she is not writing, she enjoys reading, art, music, outdoor exercise, and all things Celtic and Renaissance.

Home Is where Your Web Site Is

"The new information technology, Internet and e-mail, have practically eliminated the physical costs of communications."
Peter Drucker

In today's digital age, having a Web site is vital for any business. Many consumers choose to access a company and find out information about it online before venturing to the store or picking up the phone. The Internet is fast and convenient — two reasons that have caused it to become a necessity today.

Having a Web site can make the smallest businesses able to

compete with the largest businesses online. No one can see how tiny your business is through your Web site. You can operate from a closet in your home, and no one will know. Likewise, you could be operating from a skyscraper, and no one would know.

If you do not already have a Web site, obtaining one is an easy process. You need to find a domain name and purchase it from a site, such as **godaddy.com** or **register.com**. You can often purchase the name for less than $10 a year. You also need to purchase hosting space, which you can do through these or similar Web sites. The amount of space is dependent upon the amount of information you wish to provide to your consumers. However, this, again, is inexpensive.

Bright Idea

A Web site can launch your business into the forefront of consumer attention, putting you on equal footing with the top businesses in the world.

Once you have the name and the space, you need to create your Web site. **Godaddy.com** has a Web site developer, but you can also use professional tools, such as Adobe Dreamweaver, Adobe GoLive, or Microsoft FrontPage, which allow you to easily craft a professional Web site.

The most important part of your Web site is the home page. This is the first page that consumers see when they come to your Web site. If your site takes too long to load, they might go away. If your Web site is disorganized, they might go away. If your Web site is not visually pleasing, they might go away. This is why it is important that you make an effective home page so that visitors stay and learn more about your product or service. Most often, simpler is better.

When setting up your Web site, always have a link from every page back to your home page. Web visitors get annoyed and leave if they cannot easily navigate your Web site.

Writing the Home Page

The first step in creating an effective home page is to be conversational. Write like you are talking to your consumer. It does no good to show your massive vocabulary by using 20-letter words that no one understands without the help of a dictionary. Write in a language that your consumer can understand. Writing to 18-year-olds is much different from writing to 60-year-olds. Today, everyone wants to be considered unique and wants customizable products. With millions of people surfing the Internet, it is often not possible or cost-effective to personalize your Web site to every visitor. However, by writing in a tone that is addressed to your target market, visitors will think you are speaking to them directly, while you are addressing the masses.

A good tip in writing conversationally is to write the way you speak. In speech, we often use contractions, so do not be afraid to put those on your Web site. We also use sentence fragments. Again, do not be afraid to use those. Fill your Web site with emotion instead of making it a bland page.

You do not want your home page to look like an advertisement. More consumers are becoming immune to ads, especially the younger generations. They find themselves not trusting what advertisements are saying, and they would rather hear the information about a product or service from a friend. When they come to your Web page, you want to be that friend. Craft your Web site to look like an article, and be informative, without looking like a blatant advertisement for your product or service. You can have a link to where they can purchase your product, but do not actively say in big, bold letters at the top of your page, "Buy this." It will not work.

Testimonials

Use testimonials to grab consumers' attention. Again, this lends you credibility. Testimonials also shy consumers away from the advertisement mentality, leading them into the friend mentality. They begin to see that your product or service has worked well for other people, and they start wondering if it will also work well for them. This compels them to read more.

Article Style

Make your home page look like an article you would read in a newspaper. Besides the use of testimonials, you can make the text look and read like an article. Since your consumer and Web site visitor is likely to have a short attention span, you should write this copy in the inverted-pyramid style, which is what newspapers use. This puts the most important information in the first few sentences so that the consumer can easily understand what you are talking about and make the decision to continue reading the Web site. This way, if the consumer does not read the rest of the Web page, he or she knows what it is about and can make a decision on whether to return at a later date. It is also effective in case the consumer decides to skip around and skim the Web page. The consumer will likely read the first few sentences.

Sell Benefits

A good way to begin your home page is by writing a story about the benefits of what it is like for a consumer to use your product or service. This story shows the visitor, rather than tells, how the product or service feels. These types of advertisements appeal to emotions and make the consumer want to experience the same thing as the person in your scenario.

Embed Links

Embed links in your home page copy. This links your readers to various Web sites, but best of all, you can have them navigate to other parts of your Web site as they are reading the Web copy. This is particularly useful if you are selling a product or service. You can link the consumer at several points in the copy to a page where visitors can purchase your product or service. However, do not overuse links in your Web copy, because potential consumers may find that annoying. Do not put more than one link per paragraph in your Web copy, and place them strategically.

Highlight/Bold Copy

One last idea for writing copy on your Web page is to make select portions of your text bold. If you make certain phrases bold, they stick out in your consumer's mind, and it is also a device used to inform consumers who skim the page. The consumer may not pay special attention to the words, but subconsciously, he or she picks up on them. These are called embedded commands because they make a consumer act on the specific things you want him or her to act on. For example, if you say, "Eat Guac-n-Rock Guacamole to flavor your food," you might consider making "Eat Guac-n-Rock Guacamole" bold because that is the most important idea in your sentence. Again, you do not want to overuse this technique. Try not to use bold more than once or twice in a paragraph, depending on the amount of words you are making bold. If you make most of your copy bold, the embedded commands are a moot point, because they will not stand out.

Be aware that different types of products and different businesses use different methods on their home page. If you have a business that sells multiple products, you may use your home page as a portal to the other products. If your business sells only one product, you may be more inclined to use the inverted-pyramid method of selling that product.

Take Guac-n-Rock Guacamole, for example. In creating a Web site for this company, you would want to look at what the competition is doing. No other guacamole competitor uses a sales pitch or a call to action for its Web site because it does not sell the product on the Web site. Rather, the product is sold in stores. Crafting copy for this type of selling is much different than if you sold the product yourself.

For Guac-n-Rock Guacamole, you would be more focused on having the consumer purchase the product the next time he or she visits the grocery store. Thus, your copy would need to convey that type of message.

The copy for the home page of Guac-n-Rock Guacamole may read as follows:

Headline: Now Introducing New Snack Rockin' Snack Packs

Photo: Picture of product

Copy: Does your on-the-go life style leave you searching for healthy alternatives to flavor your food? Find new Guac-n-Rock Guacamole Snack Packs at your local grocery store today. These tasty packs contain one 50-calorie serving of guacamole, perfect for dipping your veggies, topping your burger, or flavoring your burrito. Use one for yourself and give one to a friend. The possibilities for these little wonders are endless. Bring a pack home today to rock the flavor of your food.

Call to Action: Give a link to the page that talks only about the Snack Packs so that your consumers can find more information related to those packets.

Now, take a new product — Six-Pack Abs. This product is designed to chisel your abdomen and produce atypical results in as little as four weeks. The product's Web site is the only place where the product is sold. If a section is underlined, that means it contains a hyperlink. This Web site may look more like the following:

Headline: Turn Your Flab into Six-Pack Abs

Photo: Picture of product

Testimonial: "After my third child, I decided I needed to get rid of the baby fat once and for all. I wanted the abs I had before I had my first child. Heck, I just wanted to see my abs again under all the fat. After four weeks using Six-Pack Abs, I have lost 9 pounds and 3 inches in my abdomen. I am surprised I can see a difference in so little time. I am pleased with the results. This product is fantastic." — Jane Doe (place a picture of Jane Doe before and after)

Copy: Tired of carrying around extra baggage in your midsection? Try Six-Pack abs today. With as **little commitment** as five minutes a day, three days a week, you will **see results** in as little as a month, or your money back. **Make Six-Pack Abs yours today.**

Sub-section: Revolutionary Waist-Cinching Technology

Copy: Work all sections of your abdomen to provide a thorough workout that continuously **produces results**. Six-Pack Abs' new technology stabilizes your body and allows you to work only the sections you need to so you get the results you want. **Get one today.**

Sub-section: A Fast and Easy Workout

Copy: Get a **complete workout** from Six-Pack Abs while you watch your favorite television shows. Use the machine during commercials for five minutes a day to get a great workout for your midsection. When finished, store it in your closet or slide it under your bed. Buy one now.

Sub-section: Shed the Inches

Copy: Look and feel great in under a month, or your money back. You will lose inches from your stomach and drop a pants size. Your clothes will fit you better than ever after using Six-Pack Abs. **Watch the pounds melt away.**

Call to Action: Get the body you have always dreamed of by **ordering now.**

As you can see, the two Web sites are different from each other, but both will produce results. You have to determine which is best for your Web site and take advantage of the style.

Link to additional information or a way to purchase the product.

Blueprint for Writing Web Copy

There is a blueprint for writing successful Web copy that copywriter Maria Veloso developed and tested. She has found that it has worked numerous times and sold millions of dollars' worth of products. You can read more about her successful Web copy strategies in her book *Web Copy That Sells*.

Step 1: Inject Emotion

By injecting emotion, you do not sound like a robot that has systematically cranked out this information for the consumer to disseminate. Instead, you sound like another human who has written information that you want the consumer to read.

Injecting emotion requires the use of strong verbs that appeal to the consumer's senses or imagination. The following is a list of questions that are injected with emotion. The emotional word or phrase is bolded to further illustrate the point.

- Do you get **furious** when you cannot write Web copy?

- Does it **frustrate** you that your business is not making money?

- **Imagine** the possibilities of a successful Web site.

What would it mean to you if you were featured on Oprah?

These questions appeal to the consumer and make him or her want to read more about your product in an attempt to satisfy these emotional inquiries. They help connect to your consumer, and emotion sells your product or service.

Step 2: Add Bullet Points, Bonuses, Guarantees, and Close

Bullets help break up your copy into smaller chunks that are easier for the consumer to digest and understand. These bullet points stand out from your other copy and give consumers the most vital information about your product or service.

Bonuses give your consumers incentive to buy your product or service. Here is an opportune time to use anything you can give the consumer for free to help sell your product or service. Consumers like free gifts. It makes them feel appreciated and special. It is up for debate whether free gifts sell more products, but it is accepted that they do.

A great part about using free gifts in your offer is that you can attach a sense of urgency to the gift. You can tell a consumer to act now before time runs out to receive the free offer. You can use dynamic date scripts to advance the deadline on the offer every day. This way, it creates the sense of urgency, but the offer is not going to expire. Dynamic date scripts can be found for free on the Internet by typing "Dynamic date script" into a search engine, such as Google or Yahoo!. A couple of Web sites that offer them are:

✍ **www.dynamicdrive.com/dynamicindex6/dhtmlcount. htm**

✍ **http://webscripts.softpedia.com/script/Forms-and- Controls-C-C/Free-Flash-Dynamic-Text-News-Scroller- 39460.html**

Guarantees help reassure your consumer when he or she purchases your product. Many companies like to offer a money-back guarantee. This helps alleviate any cognitive dissonance your consumers may feel after purchasing the product. It also lets them know that if they purchase the product and are unsatisfied, they can return it without a problem.

The close allows you to close your sale. Like in any good business presentation, a sales pitch is always ended with the close. This is what allows your consumers to purchase your product or service. You must ask for the order at the end, or your consumer will likely not purchase your product or service.

Good advice about the close is to make sure you prime the consumers for the sale throughout the copy. This can be done by adding links that take them to the order form on your Web site throughout the body copy. These "trial closes" allow the consumer to close the sale early or realize that the close of the sales pitch is coming.

If you are making your Web site look like an editorial or article, consider not having a direct link button in your navigation bar. If you provide a link here, consumers often skip your copy and go to the order form to see what they are getting themselves into and how much your product or service costs. You need to first sell them the benefits of the product or service and then allow them to make the purchase. Do not ruin your copy by providing this link in the navigation bar.

Step 3: Add Credibility

Adding credibility goes back to the idea of adding testimonials on your Web site. It allows consumers to see that the product or service has worked for other people.

You can also add interesting facts that are related to your product. This piques consumers' interest in what you are offering. Be sure to back up your facts by providing the sources, which will lend more credibility to your Web site. Make sure, however, that you know your sources and that they are reliable. Do not give false information, or it will hurt your product or service. Although Wikipedia may seem resourceful, and to a degree it is, it can be altered by anyone. The information it contains may not necessarily be true.

Step 4: Add Psychological Devices

You can incorporate numerous psychological devices into your Web site. For starters, provide reasons why consumers should purchase your product or service. This strategy provides a reason that the consumer needs to buy your product or service. If you provide a reason, no matter how silly it may seem, a consumer is more likely to purchase your product or service.

Another psychological device that works wonders for getting people to click from one page to another is the cliffhanger. A cliffhanger compels readers to keep clicking to see the information, because they have to know it. It is much like what TV scriptwriters do when they end the season of a show. They give you a cliffhanger to make you come back the next season. You wait around during the off-season, contemplating possible scenarios, and you cannot wait until the season premiere airs so that you can have all your questions answered. Writing copy for your Web site is no different, except consumers do not have to wait for months for the answer. All they have to do is go to the next page.

There is also a psychological device called the Zeigarnik Effect. Limit your information to one topic so as not to confuse your reader or produce information overload. In essence, keep the information on your Web site short, simple, and straightforward.

There are additional psychological devices you can use to enhance your Web site. Well-known copywriter Joe Sugarman details additional psychological devices used in advertising, which you can read about by visiting **http://www.psychologicaltriggers. com**. When you find a psychological device that works for you and your product or service, you have a winner.

Step 5: Take Rational Words and Replace Them with Emotional Ones

This goes back to the idea of using simple words. Your left brain is analytical and wants to use larger, more complex words to make your product or service appear more prestigious. However, your right brain uses smaller, more conversational words that appeal to the emotions. Here, again, it is better to appeal to your consumers' emotions.

Here is a small list of word substitutions.

    Instead of "donate," use "give"

- Instead of "purchase," use "buy"

- Instead of "elderly," use "old"

- Instead of "combat," use "fight"

- Instead of "prevent," use "stop"

The difference in the words allows a consumer to quickly understand their meaning and not think too much about what you are trying to say.

If you are unsure of how to substitute the right words or do not know the right words to substitute, you can always go to **www.paulgalloway.com/cgi-bin/emotional_words.cgi** and enter your Web site URL. This Web site shows you the rational words in your text and then gives you the emotional words to replace them with. These are in red so that you cannot miss them. You do have to enter each individual Web page on your Web site; do not only enter the home page and expect to have every page on the site analyzed.

Another tip when reading through your copy is to replace the word "if" with "when." This suggests they have already purchased the product. When a consumer is reading the copy, he or she will have already been sold the product on a subconscious level.

Bright Idea

Replace the word "if" with "when" to imply they have already purchased the product.

Beyond Your Home Page

Your Web site should have more than just one page. Use other pages to deliver different messages or communicate different ideas. This will help break up the content that you show on your home page and make the Web site more easily navigable by consumers.

You should have links to the different pages of your Web site either in a side bar or at the top of your Web site. These links need to be displayed on every page. Check them on a regular basis to make sure they are working — no one wants to run into a dead link. Also, make sure that every page links back to the home page.

About Us Page

Make sure your business has an "About Us" page. This important page is where you list information about your business, including its history and its key employees. This page should be personable. It is a chance to let the consumer get to know you better. It also helps establish that you are a real business operated by real people and not just a Web site.

Try and connect with the consumer here. They are interested in you and in your business. Do not make it seem like you have just copied this information from another place. Again, write this conversationally. If possible, try to get quotes from the president of the company or from some of the other important business people to put on the Web site. Be funny; be witty; be human.

Be sure to tell your company's history. You can use a schedule of progression to show where your company originated and where it is now. Show how the company has grown and tell where you want it to be in the future.

Mission/Values Page

Many businesses have a separate page devoted to their mission statement and their values, although some companies list this information on the "About Us" page.

If you have this as a separate page, list your mission statement and then show ways how it has influenced your business' operations. A good way of doing this is to list the various charity work that you have done.

Upcoming Events Page

Having an upcoming events page is a way for you to connect with your customers and tell them where you will be in the future. This type of page is not necessarily a fit with all businesses, but if you have a business that does outside activities and promotional events, this is a good page to have so that consumers can easily locate this information. Good things to put on an upcoming events page are trade shows you will be participating in and press releases.

Blogging Page

Many businesses are starting to use blogs to more readily update information about the business. Chapter 12 is dedicated to writing effective blogs.

Other Product Pages

If your business sells multiple products, it is a good idea to have separate pages dedicated to each one. This will help the consumer synthesize the information.

Contact Us/Locate Us Page

This page is often short. It includes contact information so that your consumers can easily reach you if they have questions, comments, praise, or criticism. If you have a brick-and-mortar operation, you can also list the location of your establishment.

Summary

The home page of your Web site is one of the most important pieces of copy you will write for your business. This needs to be written casually, in a conversational tone, and with action verbs. It needs to have a way to purchase your product and additional information about the product. Creating bold and hyperlinked text helps sell your reader. Keep the site easy to read and navigate, and let your words sell your product.

Bright Idea

Let your words sell your product.

A Final Note

If a consumer wishes to leave your Web site, let him or her leave. Do not have a script on your Web site that causes a consumer to be unable to use the back button. Though you want people to stay on your Web site, they have other priorities that they need to take care of. If you trap them there, they will become frustrated and will likely not return.

Do not have a pop-up when they try to leave, asking why they are leaving. Although it may seem like a good idea to ask the consumer why he or she wishes to leave your Web site, it only annoys them. It is often not your Web site that makes them want to leave, but rather, they have other things to do of and cannot stay any longer.

Bright Idea

If consumers wish to leave your Web site, do not try to keep them there with scripts and pop-ups.

These two tactics result in bad publicity about your Web site due to negative word-of-mouth advertising. Consumers will tell their friends not to go to your Web site because it is annoying. Their friends will trust them and then tell their friends not to go. You will miss out not only on the first customer's sale, but on several other potential consumers as well. By allowing consumers to leave your site freely, they will not have any negative thoughts about your business and may return in the future.

Behind Your Web Site

"That's what they (words) say, but that's not what they mean."
Jack Shepard from *Lost*

If you thought the writing of your Web site ended at the copy that consumers see on the screen, you are wrong. Though writing for consumers is most important, you must also write for search engines.

Search engines such as Google and Yahoo! crawl the Web, looking for key words, and then they rank sites in their searches. For example, if you search for "guacamole," the results that you see have been searched by these search engines for the key word "guacamole," and the results are listed in order of importance. We will get into Google and Yahoo! more in a later chapter.

Your copy on your Web site should be littered with the key words, but you also need to make sure they are included in the code. The code is what makes up your Web site. If you use Dreamweaver or other Web site design software, you may never see the code. However, if you view the code, you can see what is written. To see the code for your Web site, go to your Web site, right-click your mouse, and click on "View page source." This shows you all the code for your Web site.

Start Thinking Like a Search Engine

Search engines such as Google or Yahoo! decode the Hypertext Markup Language (HTML) code on your Web site and determine certain key words that are associated with your Web site. Thus, it is unlikely for a search result to display Web sites that do not contain the word searched for.

Once a search engine crawls through the vast amount of Web sites on the Internet, it determines the relevance of the key words based on different criteria. One of the main criteria is key word prominence, which determines how high up on the page your key words appear. Do not, however, saturate the first few paragraphs of your Web site with key words. Having too many will work against you, because search engines will label it as key word spam and it will hurt your search engine results.

Bright Idea

If your Web site contains an excessive amount of keywords, search engines will likely determine your Web site to be spam and ban it from search engine lists.

It is difficult to write for all the criteria of search engines, because the criteria for search engine algorithms is constantly changing. Keeping up with this information is a must; however, it is difficult to do because this information is often proprietary.

Determining Your Key Words

If you are going to write for search engines, you need to determine what key words you want to include in your Web site. Here, you want to think like consumers and create a list of several key words they might search for.

Guac-n-Rock Guacamole, for example, may determine the following list of key words:

- Guacamole
- Avocados
- Dips
- Condiments
- Sauce
- Green

The Web site writer would need to sprinkle these key words throughout the site copy. This will allow for a greater search engine result when a consumer searches for one of the words.

Writing the Code

Code is a hidden language that tells your Web site how to

function. You need to be sure to thoroughly develop and write meta and descriptive tags. Search engines read these tags and help link consumers to your Web site.

Meta Tags

To optimize your Web site for search engines, you need to have your key words written in the code. Here, you need to use meta tags. Search engines pick up on meta tags when they crawl the Web. You should enter several key words that you want associated with your business. For example, Guac-n-Rock Guacamole would include the previous list of words as meta tags. However, you also want to consider consumers and think of any misspellings they might make in using the search engine. For example, someone may not type guacamole correctly, so you should incorporate common misspellings of the word, such as guacamole or guacamole. You do not want to include too many misspellings, but you may want to list a few. Given the previous list, you may want to incorporate common misspellings for guacamole, avocados, and condiments.

To write meta tags, go to your source code, which you can find in whichever program you used to develop the Web site. To write meta tags, use the following string of code.

<meta name="key words" content="guacamole, avocados, dips, condiments, sauce, green">

Make sure that you fill in your key words within the quotation marks and close it with the > symbol. Also make sure that you do not use an excess of key words, or you will overload the search engine.

Descriptive Tags

Take advantage of your descriptive tags to better use search engines. This tag describes what your Web site is about. When you search for a company using a search engine, the results that are displayed contain brief descriptions of the Web site. Be succinct yet thorough here. Make sure that your description gains the consumer's attention and makes him or her want to visit your Web site.

Writing descriptive tags in the code is much the same as writing meta tags. Guac-n-Rock Guacamole may decide to have the following descriptive tag:

<meta name="description" content="America's favorite guacamole. We have a product line of six flavors, including our new spicy guacamole.">

What you write for your descriptive tag is what will appear under your Web site in the search engines' listings.

Determining Your Key Words

If you do not know what you need to include as key words, the best place to find them is on your competitors' Web sites. Right-click the page and select "View page source," and you can see the code that was used to write the Web site. Look at their meta tags and descriptive tags to see what key words they are using. You may determine that their key words are worth using, too, so that your Web site will appear alongside theirs. You may also determine that other words are better suited to your business which they are not using. Including these words will increase visibility of your site in the search engines.

You can also use your knowledge to view other Web sites that you often turn up in a search result. View the key words and form a hypothesis on why a Web site is ranked high by search engines. You can use this strategy in further optimizing your Web site. The more you know, the better you can improve your business' visibility.

For more information about how you can further optimize your Web site for a search engine, read *The Ultimate Guide to Search Engine Marketing: Pay Per Click Advertising Secrets Revealed* by Bruce C. Brown, published by Atlantic Publishing Company.

Case Study: Bruce C. Brown

Gizmo Graphics Web Design

How long has your business been in operation?

Gizmo Graphics Web Design has been in business since 1998 — we just hit our ten-year anniversary. We can be found on the Web at **www.gizwebs. com**.

How long have you been using search engine optimization (SEO) marketing for your business?

As a Web designer, we incorporate SEO marketing techniques into all of our Web design projects, as this is an essential component to the success of a well-rounded marketing and Web design/optimization plan. We focus on the design and SEO techniques as equally important components of the Web design, deployment, and marketing package.

Did you notice a change in business after you began using SEO?

From our perspective as a service provider, there has not been much of a difference. The obvious effect is upon clients who have come to us with previously deployed Web sites who have not used SEO techniques in their current design. SEO will not change your world overnight (you will not see a massive influx of Web site traffic as you employ SEO into your Web site); however, over time, you will see incremental improvements in search engine visibility. SEO visibility, combined with a well-designed, easy-to-navigate, and relevant Web site, will increase quality Web site traffic.

Case Study: Bruce C. Brown

What key words work best for SEO?

The "key word" for integrating key words into SEO optimization plans is "relevance." There are no magic key words, as they change substantially based on individual site content; however, your key words need to be relevant to your Web site's products, content, and purpose. Effective key words will increase SEO visibility, as those key words are indexed and searched by the casual Web surfer. Delivering effective key words that are directly relevant to your site content is a critical component of SEO optimization.

Do you use SEO in combination with an advertising campaign?

Absolutely. If you are considering e-mail advertising, pay-per-click (PPC) marketing, or other types of campaigns, key word integration is critical. Again, they need to be relevant to your content and Web site purpose to be effective. In my book *The Complete Guide to Google Advertising*, I have an entire chapter devoted to key words and key phrases.

What do you find works best with SEO?

A well-designed Web site that is content-rich and has relevant content and also provides site visitors the information they seek quickly, efficiently, and effectively. Use of other marketing and advertising techniques will round out your advertising portfolio to maximize the effectiveness of your Web site.

Has SEO helped increase traffic to your Web site?

Of course. It has also had a tremendous impact on our clients. Let us face it: Web sites are designed to attract visitors. If you have a Web site and no one can find it, is it effective?

How do you incorporate key words on your Web site into your online copywriting?

I like to write in a manner that is easy to understand and follows the basic rules of grammar while incorporating key words into the text. It is obvious when a Web site is stuffed with key words. It often is not readable and makes no sense. If it does not make sense, I am not staying on the Web site, and most others will not either. You have to catch a visitor's attention, provide good content, and keep his or her interest, but do it in a concise, organized manner.

Have you ever had your SEO go wrong?

No, although poorly executed SEO by itself will ultimately not return the results you

Case Study: Bruce C. Brown

want. The only failures I have seen is in the expectation that SEO and good Web site copy will deliver overnight success.

What do you find to be the most successful SEO combination, for example, using key words in the content of your Web site and in contextual ads and in banner ads, and so forth?

I am not a strong proponent of banner advertisements. They had their time, but it passed years ago. I am a strong proponent of good content that is rich in key words, well organized, and provides information individuals expect to find when visiting a Web site. The use of AdWords, AdSense, and other techniques is a great way to improve SEO visibility, which is all driven by key words.

What content has worked best on your Web site?

Content that is clearly written; well organized; easy to understand; not wordy; and relevant to the products, topic, or purpose of the Web site.

Any advice for people starting to write their own key words to optimize their Web sites and advertisements for search engines?

Read my books. There are plenty of tools out there to help you evaluate your Web site content and key word effectiveness. I talk about this at length and provide links to online tools to assist you in that process.

Any advice for writing better search engine content?

Write it in plain English, following basic rules of grammar, in a clear, flowing manner that grabs the reader's attention and gets to the point quickly.

Bruce C. Brown is an award-winning author of six books: How to Use the Internet to Advertise, Promote and Market Your Business or Web site with Little or No Money, The Ultimate Guide to Search Engine Marketing, The Complete Guide to E-mail Marketing, The Complete Guide to Google Advertising, *and* Returning from War.

Send & Receive

"If you want to receive e-mails about my upcoming shows, then please give me money so I can buy a computer."
Phoebe Buffay from *Friends*

Writing for a mass e-mail list is a difficult task to do well; however, it can easily provide the greatest amount of return on your small investment, given that sending e-mail is free. E-mail marketing is like direct mail in that it is sent out to a list. Although people on the list may have requested the e-mail, they may be prone to ignore it and may never begin reading it. Many mass e-mails will be filtered through as spam, and still yet, many readers regard these e-mails as spam, even though they requested it. Thus, it is important, as in all Web writing, to gain the reader's attention from the beginning and make him or her want to read more.

Personalized and Conversational

Start by making your e-mail personal. With the help of many programs, you can address each e-mail to the individual recipient. This makes the person feel that the e-mail is targeted to him or her. Many people are not aware there are special programs to do this, and they may think you have taken the time to personally address each e-mail and feel special (people like feeling special). Others may realize such programs exist and may not find the personalization special, but make sure you take the time to impress those who would find it special.

Not only do these word-processing programs allow you to personalize the recipient's name, they also allow you to personalize parts of the letter. You may decide that people with last names starting with T-Z may appreciate your offer of "buy one get one free T-shirts" more than people with last names starting with A-S. Using these programs, you can add a new paragraph for T-Z named people that the A-S people cannot see. This also allows for greater personalization and allows you to target different variations of your market more effectively. (Note: There is no study that says people with last names beginning with T-Z will appreciate a "buy one get one free T-shirt" more than people with last names beginning with A-S.)

Here is the part where personalization gets tricky. You want to make sure you do not overdo it. Some people decide to personalize their e-mails by using a person's name. Although it may seem as if personalization would compel consumers to open e-mails, consumers may also be turned off by it because they can find their in-boxes full of personalized e-mails. If I open my in-box and see the following five subject lines from five different senders, I likely will not read any of them:

- ✐ Vickie, save 10 percent this Friday only

- ✐ Vickie, your account has been opened

- ✐ Vickie, this is your last chance

- ✐ Vickie, celebrate with us

- ✐ Vickie, open this e-mail to win

A good suggestion is to personalize the subject line to a group of people, if possible and applicable, but address the individual person in the first line of the e-mail. This would make your e-mail read something like the following:

Subject: Let me buy you lunch...

Opening Lines: Vickie, start saving. Get your free lunch coupon for XYZ restaurant by signing up for our list now.

Personalizing your e-mail is your call. Subject lines are tricky, and it may work for you to use the recipient's name in the subject line, depending on the other e-mail he or she has waiting in the in-box. Although many copywriters like the personalization, just as many hate it. Another suggestion is to personalize the e-mail if the person is expecting it from your company, but refrain from personalizing the subject line in an mass e-mailing.

Be sure to include your signature at the end of the letter, which these programs also allow you to do. If you have a writing tablet on your computer, you can write your signature in a paint program. If not, you may need to sign a piece of paper and scan it into your computer as a small image and insert it into the e-mail. Make sure, as in all letters, you also have your name typed beneath the signature so that people who cannot load graphics in their e-mail or who cannot read your signature know who is writing to them.

Once you have personalized your e-mail, take the time to make it sound more like a conversation than a sales pitch. You want to be friends with the reader. Getting the sale is not just about getting the sale; it is about offering an opportunity to your consumers and guiding them to the unique benefits that your product or service offers to help save them time and/or money.

Bright Idea

Make your e-mails friendly and conversational.

When you write like you are someone's friend, it makes anything easier to read. You do not want to show off your impressive vocabulary, and you do not want to sound like a robot. You would not use six-syllable words often in a normal conversation, so there is no need to do so in an e-mail. Likewise, you would use contractions in a normal conversation, so it is wise to also do so in your e-mails.

Writing conversationally may seem easy. Unfortunately, many people can sit down and write an e-mail to their friend, but when they go to write an e-mail to a consumer, they find themselves talking in a form of "marketese" that is lost on the consumer. Lose the corporate tone and relax. You know your product is great, so write as though you were telling your best friend about it.

Quick Tips for Your E-mails

✎ Personalize — people like feeling special.

✎ Include your signature.

✎ Write conversationally — you are the reader's friend.

✎ Do not use large words, if possible.

✎ Avoid heavy jargon.

✎ Use contractions.

✎ Do not sound like a robot.

Filters

The first goal of your e-mail should be to get past the automatic e-mail filters. Although you may be quick to say that filters are bad for your business, the opposite may be true. Filters make people feel safe; they weed out your competition's e-mail, and they are not difficult to get around if you know how. Although filters may be dismissed as annoying, they may also be doing your business some good.

Automatic filters help pick through all the mass e-mail that is sent to a consumer's in-box in hopes of alleviating any viruses that may be sent to the consumer and any "junk" that the filter does not think the consumer wants. Consumers feel somewhat protected by the filters because they have less e-mail coming in than they might otherwise, and they feel that of the e-mail they do have coming in, fewer contain harmful computer viruses, and scams. However, consumers also place their own filters in their e-mail to help sort their e-mail further, making it harder still for a business' mass e-mailing to get to the consumer. Then, if your e-mail does make it to the consumer's in-box, you have to get past the his or her personal filters, meaning he or she has to read your e-mail and decide whether it is important enough not to delete it.

Although you may be tempted to use the following words, it is not advisable, because often, automatic e-mail filters have a higher likelihood of sorting through these e-mails and disregarding them as junk. Ironically, these are some of the same words you should use on your Web site to gain attention.

- Buy

- Discount

- Free

- Money

- Opportunity

- New

- Power

- Investment

✍ Profit

✍ Sale

✍ Special

Although getting through the filters may prove challenging, the best advice is to make sure that what you are offering is relevant to the person receiving the offer. This goes back to knowing your audience.

Content

Your marketing e-mail should read like a personalized letter. We have reviewed personalization techniques; now it is time to review what you should put in the e-mail itself.

Since e-mails are often just scanned by readers, you want to make the e-mail fairly short and straightforward. The average person has to sift through hundreds of e-mails a day. He or she will appreciate it if you take that into consideration.

The basic content of an e-mail marketing piece includes the subject line, the body copy, and your URL. You can add other components if you want; however, these three items will always remain. The subject line gets you into their in-box, the body copy into their minds, and the URL into their wallets.

The Subject Line

As with most Web writing, we have the first line to consider. The subject line in an e-mail blast is what lets you in the in-box. The subject line should be direct and either inform the recipient who is sending the e-mail or say the subject of the e-mail. If you are selling pharmaceutical drugs, real estate, or select Internet sites, these businesses seem to get automatically stuck in e-mail spam services more often than others.

Effective subject lines include the following:

Reduce your rates with (auto insurance company name) — This tells me exactly who the sender is and what the subject is about. I can easily make the decision on whether I want to open this e-mail. If I am in the market for auto insurance, I know that I can look at this offer.

Happy New Year! Extra 15 percent off your order from (department store) — This also tells me who the e-mail is from and what the company is offering. If I want to go shopping at that store, I will want to open the e-mail and print out my coupon.

View your bill online — Although this e-mail does not tell me who the sender is, the sender's name is clearly displayed in its e-mail address, so there is no question there. The subject is to the point and tells me my bill is ready to view online if I would like to log into my account and see it.

How to save money on almost everything — This subject line grabs your attention because it is newsworthy. Most people like saving money, and if you could save money on almost anything, you would certainly try.

Vickie, this opportunity is for you — This subject line piques my interest. I want to know what the opportunity is, especially since it is addressed to me. Also, the word "this" makes me want to know what "this" is. The word "this," along with the words "here," "about," and "your," is known to trigger the interest of readers and make them want to know specifically what is being discussed.

Vickie, we would have asked you if... — This subject line grabs my attention because I want to know what you would have asked me. Having a subject line that is an incomplete thought or one that ends in an ellipses creates a sense of tension for the reader and makes him or her want to read more.

These subject lines can grab the attention of the reader. Even if the reader does not choose to open the e-mail, piquing his or her interest means that he or she will likely see your business name as the sender of the e-mail. Every impression of your business counts. Perhaps seeing your name will cause him or her to choose your product when he or she has a need for it in the future.

Quick Tips for Subject Lines

Make your subject line short and direct. Leave no question as to who you are, or the recipient will think the e-mail is spam. If you do not say who you are in the subject line of the e-mail, make sure you are easily recognizable by your e-mail address. An example here would be an e-mail subject line that reads, "Save 20 percent on your next online purchase," from the sender "HomeStoreOffers@homestore.com." This allows the recipient to know who the e-mail is from, even though that information is not displayed in the subject line.

Make sure the e-mail address you are using sounds professional.

Do not send an e-mail from Hotgurl76@yahoo.com for your business. This will look like spam, and the recipient will not open it. Most businesses that I have received e-mail from title their e-mail name with their company name. So if your company name is Guac-n-Rock Guacamole, a good e-mail name would be guacnrockguacamole@guacnrockguac.com. Keep one e-mail address for your e-mail marketing needs. You can always have separate e-mail accounts for employees and sales.

Bright Idea

Subject lines are often the hardest part of copy to write. Take extra time with them to ensure consumers read your e-mails.

Make a subject line newsworthy. When you write a subject line like a headline to capture attention with a specific point, you will often be able to skip by the filters because you are less concerned with selling your target audience a product or service. Think about what you would want to read, and then try to come up with a subject line based on that.

Try to avoid using words that will trigger e-mail spam filters. Do not lower your chances of the consumer reading your e-mail even further by having your e-mail blocked.

The Body Copy

What is the purpose of your e-mail? The body of the e-mail is where you get to the point. This purpose needs to come across early in the e-mail, often within the first two paragraphs. It should tell the who, what, where, why, when, and how of the e-mail. This will allow the recipient to know what the e-mail is about without having to read it all. You may think this sounds contrary to sending the e-mail in the first place; however, when people are flooded with hundreds of e-mails a day, they are not going to take the time to read each one. By placing your important information in the beginning, it is more likely that they will read it and know what is going on instead of never figuring out the purpose of the e-mail to begin with.

Keep the e-mail text short and relevant. You do not want to bog down the recipient with a long, drawn-out e-mail that asks for more of his or her time than necessary. Say what you need to say and end it.

There are three different types of e-mail blasts: promotional, discounts and special offers, and informative newsletters. Each of these types alters the body copy in small ways to fit its special needs. The following sections walk you through the body copy that you will find in these different e-mails. Many of the techniques you find in one can easily apply to the others.

Promotional E-mails

Promotional e-mails are sent to promote your business or service. They are short and to the point and tell the consumer what your business is about and what benefits you can offer them over the competition. As with all copy, you want to grab the reader's attention and sustain it throughout the e-mail.

Keep the e-mail short and to the point. You want to provide consumers with interesting information about your product or service, but be aware that they have other things to do than sit at their computer and read about your offer. Keep your paragraphs short because this makes it easier for the consumer to read.

Provide hyperlinks in your e-mail. People who are interested in your product or service and want more information can click these links to find out more. Make sure the links go directly to where the consumer can purchase your product.

Discounts and Special Offers

Discounts and special offers provide products at a discounted rate or offer something special for a limited amount of time. These e-mails are often done to increase sales and contain little information. You tell what your discount or offer is, and then you offer a link to your Web site so that the consumer can easily obtain the special offer. These types of e-mails do not require much in the way of copywriting. They are more of a typical print advertisement with a link embedded in them than anything else.

These discounts and special offers provide incentives for your customers to do what you are instructing them to. Free is always a powerful offer. You can always try to provide something free, such as free shipping with a purchase order more than $100 or a small free gift. You could also say that people who sign up for your e-mail marketing offers between August 1 and September 1 will be put in a drawing to win $500. Not only do these offers lure consumers to your Web site, they also allow you to collect valuable information about your consumers, such as where they are from, their age, and their sex. Collecting this information helps you see who is buying or who is interested in your product.

However, if you make the offer, make sure you follow through with it. Consumers do not like to be misled, and they will not tolerate false information. Not only is it a crime, it also will come back to haunt you with bad publicity and negative word-of-mouth advertising.

Your discount or special offer e-mails may contain large photographs of what you are offering. Make sure that the photographs load quickly and do not take up too much of the recipient's bandwidth. This is important for keeping the consumer's attention. Consumers do not want to wait on your sales pitch. If you have graphics in your e-mail, keep them to a minimum, and make sure you check them on various Web-based e-mail platforms (such as Hotmail, Yahoo!, and Gmail), different computers (Mac or PC), with different browsers (Internet Explorer, Firefox, and Safari), with different e-mail platforms (Outlook and Outlook Express) and to see how quickly they load and what they look like before you send them out to your mass audience.

For example, if you were selling flowers and had a discount that is good for the next week, you might say the following:

> *Give Celebration. Make someone's graduation special. Fleur's Flowers is offering 20 percent off all fresh flowers from May 11-15 only. Order today to receive our special rate, and have your bouquet delivered by graduation.*

This e-mail would likely have a photograph of a bouquet relevant to graduation displayed so that the consumer can see what he or she will be purchasing.

Make sure you have a link to your Web site somewhere in the e-mail. This is vital for any e-mail marketing letter; however, when you are selling something, you want to make it easy for the consumer to find your product and purchase it. The link should take the consumer directly to the part of your Web site that is offering the special deal. Make it as easy as possible for consumers. They will appreciate the time saved.

Informative Newsletters

Informative e-mails are newsletters — some can be called e-zines — that contain updates on how a business is doing or special events that are coming up. They can also contain articles on subjects relevant to the business. These e-mails look like small newsletters that you may receive in the mail — not to be confused with business catalogs of merchandise.

You may ask, "Why bother sending an e-mail blast if the purpose is not to sell?" The answer is that you want to build a rapport with your consumers. Think of them as your friend. If you are friendly and provide them with information they want, they are more likely to think of you in the future and keep coming back to you. Although you may not make a sale initially, the word of mouth provided by the consumer (and their future purchases) will come back to reward your business in the long run. Plus, e-mail is free, so you are not wasting money by sending it; you are just putting extra time and consideration in it for the consumer's sake.

The First Line

Everything you write is always about getting to the first line. In an e-mail, you want the first line to be fascinating. Start the first line by addressing the recipient by name. This adds a personalized tone to the e-mail and makes the recipient feel like your business knows him or her.

Since you are sending an informative e-mail as more of a courtesy than to get a sale, take the time to build rapport with the consumer. Use the first two sentences as an ice breaker that is somewhat relevant to your business. For example, if you are the chief executive officer (CEO) of Guac-n-Rock Guacamole and have recently taken a trip to Mexico to tour the avocado farms, you might mention this in the first two sentences of your e-mail; just remember to be succinct:

> *Vickie, I recently returned from Mexico. The weather was hot, but it sure made for some great avocados.*

The Body

Put the most relevant information or article near the beginning of the e-mail and then repeat it in a shorter fashion at the end, similar to the inverted-pyramid style of writing that journalists use. Consumers likely will not read every word of these e-mails, especially if they are long. They will, however, be most likely to read the beginning and scroll down to read the end.

You want to write these e-mails conversationally. They are used to establish a certain amount of rapport with the consumers. You are not trying to sell them anything but instead are offering them advice and information they may not otherwise know. You want to be their friend in these e-mails. Make them laugh; let them learn. However, stay on point and keep your e-mail relevant to the consumers.

To make the e-mail more relevant, you can always make important words or phrases bold so that they stick out in the reader's mind. This is a similar technique to the one discussed in building your Web site. Also, you can provide the reader with direct links to relevant information on your Web site and external links, where they can learn more about information you discussed.

Bright Idea

Keep your consumer in mind when writing and designing your e-mail marketing piece.

Keep your e-mail focused on one topic. However, if you opt to have more than one topic, make sure your e-mail is easy to navigate. Try breaking up some of the copy with subheadings or graphics.

Informative e-mails may contain graphics. However, like in sales e-mails, you need to make the graphics small and easy to load. A consumer will not spend five minutes loading an e-mail, no matter how fancy it looks and no matter whom it is from. Keep the consumers' ease of readability in mind and consider the time they are spending on your business. Always appreciate the consumers.

Make sure you discuss benefits with your consumers. The more they find your product or service beneficial, even if indirectly, the more they will be apt to purchase it.

Another important element of an informative e-mail is providing a link to your Web site. Give your consumer the opportunity to purchase your product or service. Though you are not selling anything in this e-mail, you want consumers to be able to find you on the Web. By providing a link to your Web site, you are allowing the consumer to access your site and find more information. When the consumer visits your Web site, it may also turn into a sale for you — one you did not have to pitch. Always provide a link to your Web site anywhere you possibly can. If you provide a link within the story, make sure you link the customer to the page of your Web site that is the most relevant to the story instead of having the consumer start at your home page and search your site to find the information he or she wants. You should still provide a link to your home page at the end of the e-mail.

A good example of an informative e-mail is by Mary Larsen Designs, a sample of which is shown here. It shows how to keep an e-mail interesting and short, while offering informational tidbits that the reader might find useful. It includes small graphics that help add a better design quality to the e-mail yet are still easy to load. Finally, it ends with Mary's signature and provides a link to her Web site.

Sample Newsletter

MARY LARSEN DESIGNS

EVERY HOME HAS A STORY TO TELL

Mary Larsen Designs and Grow Your Design Biz.com

March 2007

Hello!

Time is flying and things are changing fast — I really should do a better job of keeping in touch and keeping you up with all that is new!

Sample Newsletter

As I mentioned last month — Larsen-Trochlil Designs is now Mary Larsen Designs. I haven't re-launched my current Web site — but I have added a new Web site that features the new name and logo — **www. GrowYourDesignBiz.com**.

 This Wednesday — the 28th — I will be a featured speaker at the Stein Mart at Cary Crossroads for its Spring Boutique Week. I will be sharing tips for your personal design projects and how to shop for accessories for your home. I picked the lunch hour so more of you hopefully can attend — 11:15, 11:45, and 12:15 — stop in and join me if you can!

In the meantime, please let me know if there is anything that I can do for you or your friends and family.

Read on!

Redesign and Real Estate Staging Classes

 As I mentioned earlier — finally I have launched the training piece of my business. This is for those of you who have asked me in the past to please teach or train others how to get started in the field of redesign, redecorating, and real estate staging — so this is for you!

The first class is the week of April 23–27 — and yes! You will learn everything you need to know to launch your own business! The next class is May 14–18, and classes continue throughout the year. You will do redesign work in four different homes, as well as learn "the business of the biz."

I am very excited to share what I know and help bring you along to develop your own design business dreams. Click on the link below to see the class details.

<u>Redesign and Real Estate Staging Classes From Mary Larsen Designs</u>

Follow-up to My Extreme Makeover: Home Edition

I hope you all had the chance to see the Riggins family home that aired on *Extreme Makeover* on January 21. I received great notes from over 60 people wishing the family well — and I am quite sure that the Riggins family is pleased with the results.

I was fortunate enough to have the drapes that I designed and constructed actually featured both on the show and on the *Extreme Makeover* Web site! You can see it by cutting and pasting the link below into your Web browser: **http://abc.go.com/primetime/xtremehome/featuredsears414.html** and enter "Riggins family"!

The drapes were part of the dressing room castle for the little girl, and it was a really big hit! Click below for the complete story and pictures from the show.

Mary Larsen Featured on *Extreme Makeover: Home Edition* — Full Story

If you know anyone who is thinking about getting into the design business, please send him or her to my Web site, **www.GrowYourDesignBiz.com**. I will be more than happy to talk to him or her and see how my classes can meet his or her needs.

Have a fabulous spring! And as always, let me know if you need anything or if there is anything I can do for you!

Warmest Regards,
— Mary
e-mail: mary@marylarsendesigns.com
phone: 919-773-1445
Web: **http://www.MaryLarsenDesigns.com**
Feel free to forward this newsletter to a friend.

The Visuals — More Than Just Graphics

Your consumer will always judge your e-mail by how it is presented. Make sure your text is legible and easy to read. Using all caps is not easy to read and is perceived as yelling. If you decide to use all caps, remember to do so sparingly and only when you need emphasis. A better way to go about creating emphasis on certain words is to italicize or bold them.

Make sure your font is readable. It is often best to stick with a basic font, such as Arial or Times New Roman, that people are used to reading. This makes your e-mail easier to read and saves a consumer's time. Also, make sure your font is not too small nor too large. The font size in this paragraph is 12 point, which is easy for most people to read. Sizes smaller than this are not recommended. You can always use a larger size, depending on your needs; just make sure your text is not overlapping or taking up the entire screen.

Visually, you want to make sure to use wide margins and not have any odd-looking breaks or text wraps. A good rule is to limit your characters to about 50 or 60 per line. In addition, the easiest and fastest color scheme to read is black text on a white background.

When applying graphics, make sure they are easy to load in a short time. Consumers will not wait for the e-mail to load just so they can read about your product or service. The faster your e-mail loads, the better off you are and the less likely you are to lose consumers' attention. If you use e-mails that contain heavy graphics, you may want to test them on different connection speeds (dial up, DSL, cable) to see how quickly they load.

The use of rich media, which is the use of audio and video, is starting to gain popularity. Although this type of e-mail campaign can be successful, it also can hurt you, because not everyone's computer and connection speed can handle such heavy graphics. Also, you may be blocked by filters because they perceive the file as containing something harmful, like a virus. Using rich media can also be expensive — anywhere between $5,000 to $10,000 or higher — and if you are a small business, this may not be cost-effective or even an option.

Tying Things Together

The first rule when you finish writing an e-mail marketing piece is to remember that you are not finished. Proofread the piece multiple times to make sure you have not made any errors. Do not rely on your spelling checker because it does not catch every mistake you may have made. Take, for example, the following two sentences:

- ✍ Eye halve wrote this four you're knowledge.

- ✍ To many mistakes happen in you're e-mails.

Both of these sentences show up without error on a spelling checker. Although the first sentence may be an extreme example, it shows that you can type homonyms, and as long as they are spelled correctly, the spelling checker will not help you. The second example is more realistic. "To" should be "too" and "you're" should be "your."

Make sure you use the right tenses and the right words. Using the wrong spellings happens to everyone, even large corporations.

Last week, I was at Hooters and noticed the typo of "it's" instead of "its" in its menu — a costly mistake to correct indeed.

If you send out an e-mail marketing piece that is riddled with errors, whether large or small, your consumers will find your business to be unprofessional. After all, if you cannot take the time to proofread a piece you are sending them, what makes them think you will take the time to get their order right?

Bright Idea

First impressions mean a lot. Proofread your piece multiple times to prevent errors.

As with all e-mail marketing blasts, check your e-mail from a variety of different e-mail platforms and computers to make sure the e-mail loads quickly and looks like it is supposed to. Double and triple check to make sure all your hyperlinks work accurately. It would be a wasted effort to send out an e-mail that had the words jumbled or that takes ten minutes to load because you did not check it. The knowledge you will gain from putting yourself as the consumer is priceless. Take the time to test your e-mail, and reread it to see what you can learn so that you can make the e-mail reading experience as easy as possible for the consumer.

You want to find your ideal sending frequency. A suggestion would be about twice a month, with one e-mail being either a promotional or a discount/special offer and the other being longer and informative. This will help to ensure you are not annoying consumers or inundating their in-boxes with your offers.

Make sure you have an opt-out message contained in every e-mail you send. This is the law, which will be discussed in depth at the end of this chapter. This should be a statement such as the following:

> *"Guac-n-Rock Guacamole respects your time and privacy. If you do not wish to receive any further e-mail about our company and products, please reply to this e-mail with the subject 'unsubscribe,' and we will remove you from future mailings. You can always stay up to date by visiting us online at www.rocktheguac.com."*

There is no one assured way to write an e-mail for your consumer. What works well for one company may not work well for another. You have to discover what works best for you and go with it. Just know change is constant, especially on the Internet, and you want to keep up with your consumers or you will be the one to lose.

E-mail Laws

Although the Internet is largely an unregulated medium, e-mail cannot say the same. The United States and other countries have created laws for e-mail marketing and advertising. Of note is the CAN-SPAM Act of 2003 in the United States, developed by the Federal Trade Commission.

Although there may be laws regulating spam in other countries, the United States accounts for roughly 28 percent of the world's spam e-mail messages; the next country coming close is South Korea, with only 5.2 percent. Spam is a large concern for everyone because some can contain a virus, a trojan program, malware, or spyware that can harm computers. The government has to protect consumers from illegitimate businesses that want to harm them, but legitimate businesses want to make sure they are not associated as spammers and should also be concerned with protecting consumers.

This act regulates any e-mail that promotes a commercial product or service. It details the requirements for commercial e-mail and the penalties. This section will provide an outline of the law, but before you start your e-mail marketing or advertising campaign, be sure that you read and fully understand it. You can find the CAN-SPAM law at **www.ftc.gov/spam.**

The law requires your advertising to be dependable and reliable. This means your advertising cannot contain false or misleading information. This is true of any advertising, not just e-mail. The CAN-SPAM Act states that you cannot display any false or misleading header information, meaning the e-mail address you send from and the e-mail you send must be accurate and identify the person sending the e-mail. You cannot use a fake domain name or e-mail address.

Your subject line must not be deceptive. You cannot say you are offering free houses to people when your e-mail is about prescription medication. This used to be a big problem with e-mails. Always be honest.

Make sure you have an opt-out link in your e-mail. This is often found toward the bottom, but it must be in the e-mail somewhere. This link provides the reader with the ability to choose not to receive any more e-mails from your company. Although you may not want to remove anyone from your list , providing consumers with this option is the law.

You can create a menu that allows consumers to opt-out of certain types of e-mail, such as sales e-mails. This will allow you to still send the consumer who opts out of sales e-mails your informative e-mails. Doing this creates a win-win situation for your business and the consumer because it saves both of you time and energy. There is no sense in bombarding the consumer with information he or she does not want.

Your business must be able to process these opt-out requests for at least 30 days after the message was sent. Once you receive an opt-out request, your business has 10 business days to process it and stop sending e-mail to that recipient's e-mail address.

Bright Idea

Keep up-to-date with FTC laws and regulations regarding e-mail marketing.

Your list of recipients is created through people signing up, or opting-in, to the list. You cannot sell any of these e-mail addresses to other companies because that violates the privacy rights of the consumers who wanted to receive e-mails from your company and not some other company.

The e-mail you are sending must also be identified as an advertisement somewhere in the e-mail. Often, you will see this information displayed at the top of the e-mail in small letters. Your e-mail should also include your physical postal address.

If you fail to comply with any of these parts of the CAN-SPAM Act, you can suffer stiff penalties. Each violation is subject to fines of up to $11,000. If your e-mail contains false or misleading advertising, you can also be subject to the laws that ban such advertising. You can find out more about those laws at **www. ftc.gov** and **www.ftc.gov/bcp/conline/pubs/buspubs/canspam. shtm.**

According to the Federal Trade Commission (FTC), you can also be subject to other laws and punishments in addition to the CAN-SPAM Act if you do any of the following:

- "Harvest" e-mail addresses from Web sites or Web services that have published a notice prohibiting the transfer of e-mail addresses for the purpose of sending e-mail

- Generate e-mail addresses using a "dictionary attack" — combining names, letters, or numbers into multiple permutations

- Use scripts or other automated ways to register for multiple e-mail or user accounts to send commercial e-mail

- Relay e-mails through a computer or network without permission — for example, by taking advantage of open relays or open proxies without authorization

- Use another computer without authorization and send commercial e-mail from or through it

- Use a computer to relay or retransmit multiple commercial e-mail messages to deceive or mislead recipients or an Internet access service about the origin of the message

- Falsify header information in multiple e-mail messages and initiate the transmission of such messages

✑   Register for multiple e-mail accounts or domain names using information that falsifies the identity of the actual registrant

✑   Falsely represent themselves as owners of multiple Internet Protocol addresses that are used to send commercial e-mail messages

Hear it from the Pros

Mary Larsen has been using e-mail marketing newsletters to aid her business since 2005. She believes the e-mail blasts have had a phenomenal effect on her business. The following Case Study details how Mary effectively uses e-mail marketing.

Case Study: Mary Larsen

How long has your business been in operation?

It opened in October 2001.

How long have you been using e-mail marketing for your business?

Three years.

Do you notice a change in business after you send out an e-mail blast?

Yes — almost without fail, when I contact my client list who has either worked with me in the past or has expressed an interest in working with me, someone responds saying they have been meaning to be in contact and can we please meet to discuss their next project. I think this type of communication with your client is the most important marketing tool a small business can employ.

What type of e-mail blast works best for you (long newsletters, short ones)?

The most effective e-mail blast is an e-mail that only has one topic in it — maybe a short note from me saying hello and then a feature article or feature promotion. However, I make sure to mix my e-mails up so that it does not seem that everything

Case Study: Mary Larsen

I send is a sales promotion. I have developed a little program called "the EMIs." ™ I make sure everything I send and everything I write is Educational, Motivational, and Inspirational — so even if you are not in a position to purchase something from me, you have gained helpful knowledge. And even though I know shorter newsletters have more impact, sometimes I just have plenty to say — so I do.

Do you write your own e-mail marketing or do you hire it out? Why do you choose this method?

I write all my own copy. I happen to write like I speak, which is great for this type of format. Several years ago, I was told my writing was too "breezy" and not academic enough — but that was when everything was in print, like a formal "white paper" or formal mailed newsletter. Luckily for me, times have changed enough that people are looking for information in a format that is easy to comprehend and relate to.– Newsletters and e-mails are the perfect format for that. Visit **www. GrowYourDesignBiz.com** and scroll to the bottom of the page to view the newsletter source I use and recommend.

In my interior design business, **www.MaryLarsenDesigns.com**, and my business of consulting with designers, **www.GrowYourDesignBiz.com**, my audience needs to know, like, and trust me, as well as know that I know what I am talking about from personal experience. I am not comfortable with passing on such an important task — communicating with my clients — to someone who does not know what I know.

Do you personalize all your e-mail marketing?

Every communication I write is personalized in some way. Maybe a short bit about what inspired me to write about a particular topic or just a reflection on what is happening with my business in regard to the topic.

Do your e-mail blasts tie in with the content on your Web site?

Yes. It is crucial that you be clear on what you are selling and why it will help your audience. Everything you do should be connected and consistent. Inconsistency only confuses your clients, and then they do not know what you can do for them.

Have people ever made comments on your e-mail blasts (like the quality, if they like what is in it)?

I often get feedback on my communication. This can be anything from a design client writing to say they loved the before and after pictures I sent out or a consulting client writing to say that the topic I wrote about inspired them to make a change in their

Case Study: Mary Larsen

business. And yes, creative types always have feedback on how a newsletter looks. The design and graphics and images I use are important.

How many people would you say are on your subscription list?

I have close to 2,000 subscribers on my combined lists.

Do you have a link on your Web site where people can subscribe to your list?

Oh, yes. On every single page.

Have you ever had an e-mail blast go wrong? What happened?

Yes, but just once, and you learn quickly. Before I moved to a company specifically designed for newsletters I thought I could send everything straight through my e-mail. Well, my list was getting bigger, and I was not aware of this, and so I sent out a newsletter and got a reply back from an e-mail hosting company saying that I was suspected of spamming people. I was mortified. My list was so big it looked like I was writing to just a bunch of e-mail addresses, and so my account was shut down for 24 hours while they investigated. I was cleared of the spam accusation, but having my business e-mail shut down and getting everything cleared up was not a fun task.

What do you find to be the most successful e-mail content?

I make sure that everything I send out fits the EMI™ format: Educational, Motivational, and Inspirational. People also like variety. So if I have a serious topic one month, like "how to child-proof your home," I make sure the next newsletter is more fun, like "decorating your mantel for the holidays."

What content has worked best on your Web site?

The clearer I am in the kind of client I want to attract, the better results I get. For example, when I first opened my design business, I thought "anyone who needs interior design help is my client." So basically, my Web site said, "if you need help with your home, I can help." Well, this is way too broad to comprehend. On **www. MaryLarsenDesigns.com**, when I told people I could help them with anything in their home, their eyes glazed over. It was too big, too much, and too overwhelming. But if I say I work with busy homeowners who do not have time to make their home as beautiful as they would like, they know I am talking to them.

On **www.GrowYourDesignBiz.com**, even though I am a small-business expert, I am targeting members of the design field. When you visit the site, the first thing you see is the availability of my book *How to Open and Operate a Financially Successful Redesign, Redecorating, and Home Staging Business*. It is clear right away that I am

Case Study: Mary Larsen

talking to people who are already in the field of design or who want to get started in the field.

Any advice for people starting e-mail blasts?

Just get started. Do not turn it into an enormous, insurmountable task. This is how simple it can be. Think of one service you offer your clients. Now think of a question — or the most common question — you are asked about that service. For example, I offer clients in the design field the opportunity to work with me on a six-month basis, with a focus on time management and increased earnings. A frequent question is "How will this program benefit me?" I might send a newsletter that says, "I am frequently asked how my six-month program might benefit a designer. Today I am going to list the three biggest results you will see after spending time with me." And then go into those details.

That is it. It is that easy. Now what service can you write about?

I also suggest you start a list of ideas. Anytime something you want to write about strikes you, write it down. It is great to be able to refer back to that list if you are ever stuck.

Any advice for writing better Web site content?

If you find writing difficult, start with talking. Pick a service you are passionate about in your business, have a friend ask you some questions about the service, and record the whole thing. Be sure to give fully developed answers. After listening to your response, you might be surprised to see you have content for several newsletters and may even be able to transcribe what you said — with a little tweaking — for your next newsletter.

Mary Trochlil Larsen is an established, nationally recognized interior decorating professional committed to developing design professionals through **www.GrowYourDesignBiz.com**. *Designing Your Success.™ She has taught decorating and business courses to women's groups and "trade only" conferences throughout the nation. Mary has been featured in trade publications as an industry expert and is a contributing writer for the* Raleigh News and Observer *and* The Cary News. *Her decorating business focuses on window treatments, room redesign, and home staging.*

Atlantic Publishing has recently released her first book, How to Open and Operate a Financially Successful Redesign, Redecorating, and Home Staging Business.

Case Study: Mary Larsen

Mary has had the distinct pleasure of working on the Raleigh 2007 home on ABC's Extreme Makeover: Home Edition. Her work was featured on the show and on the ABC Extreme Makeover: Home Edition site. She is also a featured designer in Teri B. Clark's real estate staging book 301 Simple Things.

Mary is a popular speaker with an enthusiastic, contagious spirit, and she easily shows others the possibilities for their own businesses. If you are looking for training classes or more personal consulting for your design-related business, you can find it at **www.GrowYourDesignBiz.com**. *To sign up for Mary's Marketing Minute Newsletter or to contact Mary, visit* **www.GrowYourDesignBiz.com** *or* **www.MaryLarsenDesigns.com**

Types of Online Advertisements

"Advertisements are now so numerous that they are very negligently perused, and it is therefore become necessary to gain attention by magnificence of promises and by eloquence sometimes sublime and sometimes pathetic."

Samuel Johnson

Online copywriting is not only for Web sites, though having a Web site is the best starting place for your company, since any advertisement that you have online will link the consumer back to your Web site. The Internet is home to a multitude of different advertising formats and offers one of the best attractions for any advertiser, which is the ability to track your consumers.

Possibly one of the best features of the Internet is the ability to track your advertisements' exposure to consumers. Many Web sites base advertising prices on the click-through rate (CTR), which is how many consumers click on your advertisement. However, even if the Web site charges a static price, you will still have access to the click-through rate of the advertisement. The higher the number, the more successful your advertisement is. Knowing your click-through rate helps you evaluate your advertisement during and after your campaign. You can make adjustments to your advertisements to learn what is most effective for your business.

These numbers are what help determine the success of your campaign. No matter what type of budget you are working with, these numbers will help guide you strategically. They will also be evidence to present to the person who is charge of your company's finances that your advertising campaign was a success. The figures can help guide you on whether you need to invest more money into advertising or where in your advertising campaign you need to invest more money.

You may not have taken the time to notice the differences among online advertisements you have seen. I do not mean the content of the advertisements or who the advertisements are for but rather how the advertisements are displayed on the screen. The Internet is one medium that offers multiple advertising platforms. For instance, a banner ad is not the same as a pop-up advertisement. This chapter will explore the differences, albeit sometimes subtle, among online advertisements.

The Banner Ad

The banner ad was, in the early days of the Internet's popularity, considered the most traditional and widely used online advertising platform. However, it has lost popularity as people's knowledge about the Internet and computers has grown.

Still, even though it is no longer the most popular form of advertising, many advertisers choose to use banner advertisements, especially with the rise of popularity of online in-banner streaming and rich media (these will be discussed in greater detail in this chapter).

Bright Idea

Banner advertisements have uniform measurements, meaning that it is easy to create one ad for multiple sites.

One perk about banner advertisements is that most Web sites that offer advertising use them. This allows you more efficiency because you do not have to take the time to construct multiple online advertisements in various formats. One advertisement will suffice for multiple sites, and that truly can be a time-saving advantage for your company. However, you might want to create multiple banner advertisements to rotate in and out after a few weeks, since click-through rates have been known to decline after a few weeks' exposure.

As with all advertisements, there are some tricks to conquering the banner advertisement to give yourself a higher click-through rate.

Pay attention to your copy. Make sure your messages are carefully worded. Do not make your ads verbose. Short, crisp messages can achieve high click-through rates for you. Try and address concerns; offer benefits.

Grab consumers' attention. One effective way to grab their attention is to use a new headline for your advertisement. This grabs the consumers' attention and makes them want to read more about your product or service. The best part is that your advertisement does not appear like an advertisement because it reads as if it is news.

Use color in your advertisement. This does not necessarily have to be a colored font, but perhaps a colored background or a colored image. Color will lure the reader's eye to your advertisement. However, you must also be careful with colors. For a more detailed explanation of color, see Chapter 14 on design principles.

Some banner ads with high CTRs have words such as "Click now" and "Get it here." Another design idea that is known to achieve a high number of clicks from visitors, though inadvertently, is the use of alert boxes or some Windows application status boxes.

An example could be an antivirus company using a Windows alert box saying, "Virus-like activity detected on this computer. Do you want to detect and remove virus? Yes. No." Visitors could mistake this banner for an alert message from their system and click on it.

Since banner advertisements have been around so long and are commonly used, many different banner advertisements exist.

These different types come with different positioning on the Web site, and different positioning also translates to different pricing. This means that even if you cannot afford the "best" placement on a Web site, you may still be able to afford placement elsewhere on the Web site.

A few examples of the more popular types of banner advertisements will be discussed in the following sections; however, some Web sites offer a variety of other options and can often work to fit any price range you have for your campaign. Keep in mind that though the actual size is displayed, banner ads will look much larger on your computer screen.

If you determine that one particular banner advertisement is not working for you, you may want to create a different style of banner advertisement using a different size or different page positioning.

North Banner Ad

You may already be familiar with north banner advertisements, as these are often some of the most prominent on Web sites. A north banner advertisement appears at the top of the Web page. When people refer to "banner ads," they often mean the traditional north banner advertisement.

North banner advertisements may be about 728 by 90 pixels in size. The following is an example of the typical size of a north banner advertisement.

North banner advertising may be more expensive than other banner advertising because it is one of the first things that a consumer will see on the Web site. However, it may be worth the cost for this very reason. Like with all advertisements, you want to gain the consumer's attention and you want to make sure to display your logo. The great part about banner advertising is that if the consumer clicks on your advertisement, he or she is directed to your Web site, where you can transform the interest in your product or service into a sale.

The north banner advertisements are often better suited for a more verbose advertisement because the horizontal aspect makes words easier to read. These ads are also better suited for advertisements containing larger words so that they fit across the screen rather than being cut off or chopped in half. However, you should not use too many large, hard-to-understand words in any advertisement. This would be a better option if your company's name is long or if you need a large font for your advertisement.

Towers or Skyscrapers

The best example of a tower or skyscraper banner advertisement is if you take the north banner advertisement and make it vertical instead of horizontal. In other words, these ads resemble their name. These banner advertisements can go by many different names and they come in various sizes, although a common size is about 120 by 600 pixels. The following is an example of a tower or skyscraper advertisement.

These advertisements are better suited for pictures and shorter words or phrases because you have less horizontal space to work with. Being smaller in width, they can make copy harder to read, especially if it is crammed from margin to margin.

Tower or skyscraper advertisements can be found on either side of a Web site. In English, people read left to right, which might make the positioning on the right side of the page more attractive than the left. However, Web site owners know this and may either use the right side of the page for their own purposes or may charge a higher price for the space. If your advertisement is placed on the right side of the Web site, you can compensate for the positioning by using color to draw the consumer's eye.

Square and Rectangular Banners

Square and rectangular banner advertisements provide the best of both worlds for a copywriter and art director because you have enough space to use any word you chose, with perhaps the exception of supercalifragilisticexpialidocious.

A square banner advertisement is often 240 by 240 pixels (see the following example), and rectangular banners can vary to give you more room horizontally or vertically, depending on your advertisement. No matter your dimensions, these rectangular advertisements will likely still serve as a better advertising structure for more copy (by more, I do not mean a lengthy paragraph). These advertisements also allow for larger graphics.

These banner advertisements are often located on the sides of the Web site. Depending on the Web site that you are advertising on, these may appear on the left or right side of the page. Again, the right side of the Web site may be more desirable than the left side.

In-Banner Streaming and Rich Media

Many Web sites allow in-banner streaming or rich media, which means that you can use programs such as Flash MX or Macromedia to add animation to your banner advertisements. This animation can last between 10 and 30 seconds and then go to a regular image, often your last frame. Some Web sites do not have set time limits for the animation and allow you to keep it on a continuous loop; however, this may annoy your consumers and distract them in a negative way. A good example of the continuous animation would be banner ads that instruct you to "shoot the duck" and have animated ducks running across the screen with a gun scope cross hairs across them. When consumers are trying to read the Web site for other information, seeing the scrolling ducks running across a banner may annoy them and make them not want to see anything about your product or service.

The popularity of in-banner streaming is gaining momentum. The use of animation helps gain consumer attention. It also allows you to develop longer messages that do not remain static on the page. In addition, you can add more content to your advertising and show consumers benefits rather than limiting you to telling about the benefits of your product or service.

The best thing about in-banner streaming is that the ads are dynamic and are making Internet advertising more akin to broadcast advertising rather than print advertising. Anyone can create these simple animated advertisements with the right programs. Flash MX has a free 30-day trial download from **adobe.com**. You can easily look up tutorial sites or purchase books on how to use the program and start creating animated advertisements. However, it may be best to hire someone experienced in these programs to create a more effective advertisement that looks professional. Doing this is still likely cheaper than creating any television commercial.

Making Your Banner Ad Effective

Though banner advertisements may be in a partial decline to online advertisers, the invention of in-banner streaming has helped pick up their sales. If you do not use in-banner streaming because of lack of knowledge or lack of budget, there are other ways to make your banner advertisements effective.

Pay attention to your copy. Your messages should be carefully worded and rewritten until you make your advertisements succinct and meaningful. Short messages that address the consumer's concerns or offer benefits to the consumer will achieve higher click-through rates.

Think about the verbiage you are using. If you say, "Click now," "Warning," or "Hurry," you are likely to grab the consumer's attention and make him or her want to know more. Some companies design their advertisements to look like alert boxes or error boxes seen on a computer in hopes that it will gain consumers' attention and make them think something is wrong with their computer and click the advertisement. Although this strategy has worked for these companies, it is not always nice to fool the consumer into thinking something is wrong. Stress the benefits of your product or service rather than try to fool the consumer. If you have something free to offer them, here is your opportunity. Free is always a word that piques anyone's interest.

Use color to gain the consumer's attention. Make sure the colors you use are not too garish, and make sure the advertisement is still easy to read and understand.

If possible, use in-banner streaming to make your advertisement more dynamic and eye-catching. In-banner streaming will allow you to actively engage the consumer, allow you to have a longer message, and will show the consumer benefits rather than only telling them.

Unicast Advertisements

Unicast advertisements are a type of in-banner streaming. However, this type of advertisement goes beyond simple animation programs and uses video and audio like a standard television commercial. Here, you can still use programs such as Flash to embed the video, but you will need more sophisticated computer programs to record and edit your streaming video before publication. Unfortunately, being like a television commercial means higher costs and greater knowledge needed. A small company may not be able to afford the production of such an advertisement.

This type of advertisement is growing in popularity as more people are gaining access to high-speed Internet in their homes. It is also growing in popularity for advertisers because it costs less to advertise on the Internet than it does on television.

Unicast advertising allows you to create a 10- to 30-second advertising spot that will engage the user as an interactive commercial. Essentially what advertisers are doing is creating advertising spots on the Internet that are similar, if not identical, to those advertisements that we see on television. A good example of this is by MasterCard.

MasterCard has a campaign called "Priceless Pep Talks from Peyton Manning." Some of the pep talks can be seen in commercials on television; however, those commercials also drive consumers to MasterCard's Web site. MasterCard has taken the commercials to the 30-second unicast advertising spots on various Web sites, such as Yahoo! and ESPN. The commercials on television and on the Web are the same, which cuts back on the expenses for MasterCard because it does not have to film a separate commercial for each media. To view a priceless pep talk from Peyton Manning, visit **www. priceless.com/us/personal/en/extras/peptalks/index.html**. MasterCard's Web site allows consumers to customize their own pep talk instead of seeing the same one that appears online and on television.

When your 10- to 30-second advertisement is finished, consumers have the option to play it over again. If they choose not to do this, the advertisement will remain on the page as a still image, which will still allow you to generate impressions.

Although unicast advertising is gaining popularity, especially among national multimillion dollar corporations, one must still be concerned with the fact that not every person's computer can handle the extra strain of these streaming advertisements. If someone has low processing power, or if he or she does not have a high-speed Internet connection, the ability to watch these commercial advertisements is low. If you are a small business considering this type of advertisement, think about your consumers. You want to make it easy for them to see your advertisement.

Also, although you can use audio in unicast advertisements, you must realize that not every consumer will have the audio turned on, or if it is turned on, once the audio starts he or she may turn it off. For this reason, you need to have text displayed in your advertisement and not let it all be audio. This will allow the person without speakers or the person with the sound turned off to still understand the message of the advertisement. MasterCard displays the text "Priceless Pep Talks from Peyton Manning" in the advertisement and has the words spoken aloud. Consumers can also see Peyton Manning and the MasterCard logo. Still, MasterCard runs the risk of the consumer not hearing the advertisement and getting the full message; however, the ad displays enough text that the viewer can choose whether he or she wants to see the commercial.

Although unicast advertising has its drawbacks, it has some definite advantages, too. Unicast advertising allows you to actively engage your audience. It allows you to quickly gain consumers' attention and draw them into your advertisement and message. It allows for a higher entertainment value and gives you a greater dynamic of graphics available. Unicast advertising allows for you to engage a consumer's imagination and gives you a greater amount of creativity.

Writing copy for unicast advertising may be different from other copy you have written. Here, you may be writing dialogue for actors rather than writing type. Or, you may be writing dialogue and type. You will have to frame each part of the advertisement and piece it together to form a final product.

Many of the rules of copywriting stay the same when writing for unicast advertising.

First and foremost, you want catch your consumer's attention. Have a catchy opening line, whether it be displayed text or spoken. This, again, is essential to engaging consumers and keeping their attention throughout the advertisement.

Bright Idea

Unicast advertising gives you more creativity and is a great way to interact with consumers.

Make sure you have a careful balance of copy and graphics. For unicast advertisements, you may be more reliant on graphics because they will be streaming across the advertisement like a movie. Therefore, your copy and the graphics should fit together naturally.

Write conversationally, especially if you are writing dialogue. This will seem more natural for your consumers. Read your copy aloud multiple times before you make your advertisement. If it does not sound conversational, continue to tweak it until it does.

If using printed words, make sure there are few, they convey a point, and that the consumer has a long enough time to read them before they disappear from the screen.

Make sure you have a still screen that includes your logo and a few words, likely your positioning or tag line, to go to after your 15 or 30 seconds have played. This will allow consumers to see what the ad was about and decide whether they want to play it again or visit your Web site. Having your business logo also allows you to leave a longer impression on consumers while they are on the Web site on which you are advertising.

Pop-up Advertisements

Pop-up advertisements open when you open a Web site. They are often thought of as highly annoying and aggravating. They are used with the hopes of the consumer reading them first or clicking on them (often by accident).

However, pop-up advertisements are more of a nuisance to the consumer than anything else, because they slow down many consumers' computers, and multiple pop-ups often open instead of one. Now, many Internet browsers, such as Mozilla Firefox, offer free pop-up blockers, eliminating or drastically reducing this type of advertisement.

A variation to the pop-up advertisement is the pop-under

advertisement, where instead of having the advertisement appear in front of the browser, it appears behind it. The consumer will then see the advertisement when he or she has closed the browser. A disadvantage to this type of advertisement is that the consumer has already made an active decision to leave the Internet before ever seeing the advertisement, which means he or she is less likely to visit your Web site.

Although pop-up advertisements are still in use, they are not wise to use, because they will often be blocked. You do not want your consumers to become annoyed with your product or service. Instead, you might opt for a less intrusive form of Internet advertising.

Take-Over Ads

Take-over advertisements occur when a Web site at first displays a large advertisement for a product or service, which consumers will first view when visiting the Web site. Consumers can easily close out of the advertisement; however, the entire Web site contains advertisements from the same company. This use of advertising helps brand a company or product and leave valuable impressions of the product or service in the minds of the consumers.

A good use for this type of advertising is if you have a new product or service that you want to introduce to consumers. To take full advantage of take-over advertising, you need to have a common theme among your campaign so that you can brand it across all the advertisements presented on the page to allow the consumer to easily recognize that they are all for the same product or service. This can be done by using the same tag line or positioning line, using the same colors, using the same graphics, or using a combination of these things.

Split-Screen Advertisements

A split-screen advertisement is self-explanatory. The advertisement appears on a portion of the Web page. It takes up a large amount of space that would otherwise be devoted to the Web site's content. These advertisements, however, have a higher click-through rate than banner advertisements, according to the book *Advertising Campaign Strategy* by Donald Parente.

Classified Advertisements

The classifieds are not just for your daily newspaper. Now, many Web sites offer the ability for small businesses to use classified advertising online. You can still advertise online through your local newspaper, or you can find another Web site, such as **craigslist.com**, on which to advertise.

Writing a classified advertisement online bears a strong resemblance to writing a classified advertisement for your local newspaper. First, you want to grab the reader's attention. When your advertisement is listed alongside possibly hundreds of others, you need to quickly gain the consumer's attention, or no one may ever find your advertisement. You can do this by offering something free or discounted, two easy ways to gain attention. You can also use bolded or italicized words and color (this may cost more for your advertisement), but these tricks will make your advertisement stand out from a page of gray.

Have a strong, attention-getting headline. Tell the consumer how he or she will benefit from your product, such as by saving money or increasing sales. Use buzzwords to gain attention quickly.

Your body copy will be short because you will not have much room in a classified advertisement. Promote the benefits of your product or service. What sets your product or service apart from your competitors'? Here is where you should say the difference. Let your consumer know that it is not a difficult decision to pick you over the competition.

Finally, end the advertisement with your Web site. Link consumers directly to the part of your Web site where they can find out more about what you were offering in the advertisement. Save them time and make it easy for them.

A good example of a classified advertisement is as follows:

Write Great Classified Ads

It's simple. Double your responses today.

www.easyclassifeds.com

Contextual Advertisements

Contextual advertisements are those advertisements that are text-only and that appear on a search engine page based on the content that was searched for. These advertisements are highly effective when used with proper search engine optimization techniques, which you can learn more about in Chapter 9.

An advantage of contextual advertising is that your

advertisement also appears near the link for your business' Web site, which helps establish your business' credibility to consumers. It also helps to give consumers multiple exposures to your business' name. In addition, contextual advertising is easy to use, and anyone can get started using it on any of the search engines by establishing an account, selecting key words, and determining a price. Contextual advertising works with any budget because you select what price you want, which is determined by the click-through rate of the advertisement. For example, you determine that you have a daily price limit of $15. After $15 worth of click-throughs, your advertisement would no longer appear for that day.

Perhaps the most popular contextual advertisement is that of Google AdWords. These advertisements are displayed when you search for a particular word or phrase, either in the top of the search results or on the right side of the page. You can also find other contextual advertisements on search engines such as Yahoo!, MSN, and Ask.com.

Although each of these search engines has its own specifications for using contextual advertising, all are similar. Google may be the easiest to use because it allows for multiple options and it also helps instruct you on which key words may be the most beneficial for your product or service. However, using contextual advertising on all the major search engine Web sites is easy to use and can be done by clicking on "advertising," located at the bottom of each of the Web sites.

Writing effective Web copy may seem difficult for contextual advertising because you have such a small amount of room to capture the consumer's attention. Fortunately, contextual advertising is so targeted to your consumers that you need only write the words consumers want to see. Often, you will have the link that appears first be your business' name, a catchy slogan, or a command, such as "buy our product." The sentences that follow often describe your business or what you sell. Here, you should be succinct and accurately describe your business to make the consumer visit your Web site.

For example, Guac-n-Rock Guacamole may have a contextual ad that looks like the following:

> *Rock Your Guac!*

> *Spice up your bland food with Guac-n-Rock guacamole.*

> *www.guacnrock.com*

Or, if Guac-n-Rock Guacamole is having a sale, it may choose to advertise that to get more consumer attention. In this case, the ad may appear as:

> *Try Guacamole*

> *Get 10 percent off your next Guac-n-Rock purchase by visiting our Web site today.*

> *www.guacnrock.com*

For real examples, go to Google, MSN, Yahoo!, or Ask.com and do a search for a common product, such as chocolate or DVDs. You will see several contextual advertisements appear. Study these to see which ones would make you most want to visit a Web site. Try this again with the type of product or service that you are offering and see what your competitors say in their contextual ads. This also allows you to see if your competitors are using contextual advertising and if they are using it on every search engine.

If you choose to use Google AdWords, you can visit its Web site at **https://adwords.google.com**. While there, you can have Google recommend key words for you. If you type in a key word about your product, Google will generate a list of key words and phrases that people commonly use. Google also lists the percentage volume and highest month that volume occurred in for each of the key words or phrases. Of course, if you have built your Web site using search engine techniques and key words, then you will know better than Google what key words you would need for your product or service. The following Web site will give you a better example of what key words you will want to use:

https://adwords.google.com/select/KeywordToolExternal?defa ultView=2

Again, let us take Guac-n-Rock Guacamole as an example. If you type in "guacamole" for a list of Google key words and phrases, Google recommends the following:

Keywords related to term(s) entered - sorted by relevance

Keywords	Avg Search Volume	Search Volume Trends (Dec 2006 - Nov 2007)	Highest Volume Occurred In	Match Type: Broad
guacamole			May	Add
guacamole dip recipe			Feb	Add
guacamole dip			Feb	Add
guacamole recipes			May	Add
guacamole recipe			May	Add
recipe for guacamole			May	Add
guacamole dip recipes			Feb	Add
how to make guacamole			Aug	Add
easy guacamole			May	Add
easy guacamole recipe			Oct	Add
best guacamole			Oct	Add
make guacamole			Aug	Add
guacamole calories			May	Add
holy guacamole			Oct	Add
chipotle guacamole			May	Add
guacamole nutrition			May	Add
calories in guacamole			May	Add
guacamole recipie			Feb	Add
wholly guacamole			Sep	Add

Google will also do a key word search for you if you enter in your Web site URL. Google will use only the page that is displayed in the URL, so if you have multiple pages in your Web site, which most people do, you must run them all individually. Make sure the URL has text on it and is not done completely in Flash or Macromedia. If your Web site is done completely in one of these programs, Google will not be able to find any key words or phrases because there is nothing for it to search. Google does not read images and will not be able to produce any key words or phrases based on those images.

Also, Google may not get the key words or phrases of your Web site entirely right. After entering in a page from my personal Web site, Google gave me a list of some key words and phrases that do not belong. Thus, you need to double-check everything Google says when you select the option of having the search engine determine your key words and phrases. Fortunately, Google has a part of its search where you can enter in negative key words. These are the words you do not wish to associate with your

Web site. For example, if Guac-n-Rock guacamole did not wish to associate the term "avocado" with its Web site, it could enter it in the negative key word search and then Google would not generate any suggestions related to avocados.

Google will do a scan of any Web site, making it an excellent idea for you to enter in your competitor's URL and see what key words and phrases turn up. This will further help you analyze the competition and see what it is using as key words. Although it may not sound like an advantage, you will better realize what you can do to tweak your own key word searches.

Google AdWords can be an inexpensive solution for your business and an easy way to gain Web site traffic and increase sales. Tips for you to remember when you purchase Google AdWords include the following:

- Make sure you aim for your target market. Google AdWords does not allow you much space to capture your consumers' attention, so you need to make sure you know what your consumers are searching for. Another great aspect of Google AdWords is that it allows you to target your searches by key words and by geographical area.

- Insert key words, but make sure not to cram your advertisement full of them. You do not want to go past four key words in any advertisement.

- Use your short headline to grab the consumers' attention and make them want to visit your Web site. Ways to do this are by:

- Listing your business' name upfront

- Telling readers what you want them to do (if you want them to buy, say, "buy this product")

- Using active verbs to describe your product

Be succinct and descriptive. You have a limited space to make a statement and attract consumers to your Web site. You also need to let consumers know what your business is offering so they can decide whether they want to visit your Web site.

Write in a conversational tone. You do not want the reader to know you have put targeted key words into the advertisement. Rather, write as if you were talking to someone else. It will help you gain the interest of the consumer, and it will make you sound less robotic.

Do not write in all caps. Although this may seem obvious, people often do not realize that on the Internet, writing in all caps suggests that you are "yelling" at the reader. Consumers do not want to be yelled at. Also, reading an advertisement in all caps is difficult.

Other Online Advertisements

In addition to the basic forms of online advertising previously described, advertisers have other methods they employ.

Games

One such method is embedding your brand into an online game.

Many consumers still come online to play games. A Web site that allows advertisers to develop games and have them on their Web site is **Neopets.com**. If you access their game room, you can often see games by Trix, Cheerios, The Limited Too, and other companies.

Web sites that allow users to play free games sometimes have advertisements in the game, an example is **www.popcap.com**. After the consumer gets past so many levels or plays for so long, then they will be forced to view an advertisement.

Bright Idea

Use creativity in finding places to advertise online.

The best way to have an online game is to embed your company logo somewhere in the game but not have consumers think that the game is about selling your product or service. You want to develop something that is truly entertaining for them. If they are exposed to your company logo enough times, they will be intrigued enough to visit your Web site. Consumers do not necessarily like to know that the games they are playing are advertisements.

Chats

Another way to advertise is to embed your logo in chat rooms or to sponsor online chats with people. These are not traditional advertisements and are used to gain consumer interest. Again, they should not be targeted at selling your product but rather at entertaining and gaining the interest of your consumers.

Webisodes

Marketers are responding consumers' dislike for advertisements by creating something known as a Webisode.

Webisodes are akin to afternoon soap operas in that they are often sponsored by a company. These Webisodes are short movies, approximately two to five minutes in length. They often feature a product in prime positioning, and they try to be compelling and grab the consumer's attention.

Copywriting for Webisodes will be a different experience than copywriting for other advertisements. Writing for these will allow you to use more creativity and more words. This type of writing is like a mini-movie script. You are not writing to sell your product — your product name may surface only once or twice, if at all. This is about the positioning of the product and about entertaining consumers.

Summary

Many different options for advertisements are available on the Internet. Once you have found a Web site that you would like to advertise on, look up the types of advertisements allowed and their specifications before you begin creating your advertisements. It would be ineffective to create an in-banner streaming skyscraper advertisement for a Web site that allows only static north banners. Likewise, it would be inefficient to create a rectangular banner at 250 by 400 pixels for a Web site that has only rectangular ads that are 300 by 450 pixels.

Use color where possible. This will help gain consumers' attention and attract them to your advertisement. You do not have to use color on your text, but you can use it for your background or images. Make sure you do not overdo it or use garish colors that would repel consumers.

Make sure your copy is succinct and attention-grabbing and conveys the benefits of using your product or service. Make your customer want to read and know more about your product.

Try writing an ad like a news headline. It makes the consumer want to read more about your product or service, and it looks less like an advertisement.

Make a special offer. The word "free" goes a long way on the Internet, and you should use it whenever possible. If you can get away with using it in your advertisement, then say it. It likely will increase your click-through rate; just make sure you explain the free offer in detail to the consumer once on your Web site.

Use the advantage of the Internet to convey more knowledge to your consumers by having a Web site and by linking to it in your advertisement so that consumers can click on your ad and be directed to your Web site. Make it easier for them by directing them to the page on your Web site that contains the specific information they want instead of directing them to your home page and having them search for the information.

Track click-through rates to help determine what you are doing right and what you are doing wrong. This will tell you where your advertising is most effective. If you are getting the click-throughs and hits on your Web site but you are not making many sales, you might need to tweak your Web site. If you are getting many click-throughs on Google but not on MSN, you might want to tweak your advertisement on MSN or reallocate your money to more effective channels.

In the future, the lines between television and the Internet will become blurred, even more so than they are already. Be on the lookout for more unicast advertisements, and start looking for ways now to create them. Also be on the lookout for more ways to reach your target audience without having your advertisement look like an advertisement.

Case Study: Mike Roe

What made you want to become a copywriter?

Whenever I would search eBay for "money machine," I would find some "killer MEGA copywriting course" or "super DELUXE copywriting seminar in a box" stating I could "learn from the lost masters of copywriting" how to "literally write any size paycheck" I would like. Sounded great. Unfortunately, what I have never found is a bank willing to cash those checks. So I had to devise a way for someone else to write those paychecks.

Honestly, I had always been attracted to advertising. When other kids were out throwing rocks and burning things, I was in my room/office, reading the ads in comic books and waiting for the commercials that ran between the Saturday morning cartoons. I cannot remember much about the shows I watched back then, but I can remember to this day practically everything about the commercials that paid for them, especially the slogans. Then, in my teens, I fell in love with movie poster tag lines. I like a great tag line better than a good movie.

Eventually, I graduated from Notre Dame with a marketing degree and moved to Los Angeles, where I thought it would be great to get paid to write ads and movie posters. Besides copy groupies, what could be better? Anyway, I have been an advertising copywriter now for more than 10 years, and what initially attracted me to the business is what continues to excite me about it today — it is fun and you get to work in an industry that values and rewards creativity.

Case Study: Mike Roe

What was your first assignment? How did you feel about it?

My first Web copywriting assignment was for a heart surgeon specializing in cardiac arrhythmias, specifically atrial fibrillation. How did I feel about it? Dumb! Up until then, my experience had been exclusively print copy, primarily writing comedic movie tag lines and packaging for interactive games and toys. So I had to learn a completely new industry… two new industries — the Internet and heart surgery — and fast.

But whether for print or the Web, if you hope to make a living as a copywriter, you have to be a quick study. Ultimately, writing for that heart surgeon and knowing there were people with atrial fibrillation searching the Web for a doctor who could help them possibly enjoy a better quality of life and live longer made me feel great. The feeling was short-lived, though, as I was soon asked to write Web content for plastic surgeons — back to school.

What do you know now that you wish you had known when you first started?

In advertising, you will often present several concepts to a client. When I first started writing copy, I was afraid clients, or even other creatives, would steal ideas of mine that were not selected to be used on the campaign. A coworker at the time, and a friend ever since — a successful Hollywood art director, by the way — told me that if I had only a campaign's worth of ideas, I was in the wrong business. He was right. Regarding Web copy, many years ago, I wrote what I considered to be great copy for a client's site. Although the client was happy with the copy, this was before I had learned anything about key words and search engine optimization. I was writing the site the same way I wrote for print. They are not the same.

What is the toughest copywriting challenge that you have faced?

As a freelance copywriter? Getting paid. As a full-time Web content writer, having to write about the same subject — in my case, plastic surgery — hundreds of times while ensuring that the copy is not only 100 percent unique, so as to satisfy search engines, but also informative and entertaining, so as to satisfy the reader. When it comes to writing Web copy, I have adopted a personal tag line — advertising copywriting for a new word order. That is sometimes how it can feel when you are asked to write another page about something you have written about repeatedly.

How does Web copywriting differ from traditional copywriting?

First, when it comes to traditional print copywriting versus Web copywriting, there are obvious differences as to how much you can write. With a print ad, there is room for a short headline and maybe three or four sentences; a Web page allows for 300

Case Study: Mike Roe

to 800 words. Also, whereas print ads focus primarily on the headlines, as that is all most people will read when deciding whether to invest time in reading the rest of the ad, writing for the Web is primarily about using the right key words to ensure that someone performing a search finds your client's page. With print copy, the consumer often is not hoping to find your ad. So, you try to grab their attention in just a few seconds with something that promises to fulfill some almost unknown need or desire. With the Web, the consumer is searching for you. So, you try to provide them with solutions to their problem. Finally, print copy, in my opinion, is scrutinized more, because the client is paying more money for the placement of the magazine ad or billboard or the printing of the brochure or packaging. Also, once they sign off on it, the client is going to have to live with it for a while. So, if there is a typo or the campaign proves ineffective, time and money have been wasted. With the Web, copy can be changed at any time.

Who are some of the clients you have worked for?

On the print side, I have worked with Disney, Playmates Toys, and HBO. As a Web content writer, I have worked with Leaf & Rusher Beverly Hills, Marina Plastic Surgery, Key Laser Institute, and Plastic Surgery Associates.

What is your biggest success? What copy have you crafted that you loved?

I enjoyed writing body copy for the packaging for "The Simpsons Celebrity Edition" line of toys and working on movie tag lines for the Joe Dirt poster. With regards to the Web, I wrote a series of search engine optimized episode commentaries for a nip/tuck Web site sponsored by a prestigious plastic surgeon in Los Angeles. Those were fun.

What are the best tips you have for successful Web copywriting?

To be successful in writing for the Web, you have to first be a successful copywriter. And what I mean by that is that you should read as much about as many different topics as time allows. You do not have to know much about everything, but knowing a little about several things will certainly help you in the long term. I would also recommend that you always try to write in a way that is natural for you and in a way that sounds natural to the reader. As Kurt Vonnegut recommended in *The Observer*, "Keep it simple, do not ramble, and sound like yourself." When you write for the Web, I would also suggest that you keep in mind that, ultimately, you have four clients: the person writing you that "huge paycheck," the consumer your client is hoping to reach, the search engines, and, of course, yourself. And, please, do your best to put real people ahead of the search engines, because while it is your job as a copywriter

Case Study: Mike Roe

to help consumers find your client's site, it is only half the job. You have to write in such a way that once they have searched for and found your client, they will want to stay there for a while. Last, when selecting key words, never guess.

Do you feel that it is more important in copywriting to be creative or a salesperson?

It is important to be an advertiser, because an advertiser is a creative salesperson.

www.hollywoodcopy.com

www.guysguidetoplasticsurgery.com

Mike Roe is a freelance copywriter and Web content writer living in Paso Robles, California. He specializes in tag lines but also provides long- and short-form advertising copywriting and ethical search engine optimization to a wide variety of clients in Los Angeles and San Francisco, as well as around the country, including motion picture studios, interactive gaming publishers, toy manufacturers, plastic surgeons, dermatologists, orthodontists, upscale apparel retailers, insurance companies, and luxury cosmeceutical companies. With more than ten years of experience as an advertising copywriter, Mike has written copy and provided concepts for print, TV, radio, and the Web. In 2006-2007, he wrote more than 500 pages of unique Web content for more than 30 plastic surgeons and dermatologists in 16 states. In 2008, he created the Web site Guy's Guide to Plastic Surgery for Men.

Blogging

"There's nothing to writing. All you do is sit down at a typewriter and open a vein."
Walter Wellesley "Red" Smith

Blogging is sweeping the Internet. A blog, short for "Web log," is a way to share your feelings with other people. Blogs are often thought of as shared diaries that people can post online. Although this may be true for teenagers, it is not customary to think of a blog as a diary for businesses. After all, you will not find a large audience that wants to read about a business' daily activities. Rather, for businesses, blogging has become a way of connecting to readers and sharing new information with them.

Why Blog?

Blogging allows your business to go beyond your Web site and connect with the reader on a more intimate level. In essence, it can become a blend of your Web site content and your newsletters.

Writing a blog will allow you to share your views on a particular subject that your readers may find interesting. For instance, if you are writing a blog for Guac-n-Rock Guacamole, you might find the topic of avocados interesting, so if a news story comes out pertaining to avocados, you may feel the need to write about it. You might also find yourself wanting to talk about rising food prices and how that will affect your business. If guacamole becomes an intricate part of pop culture, you may want to blog about that. If Britney Spears or Paris Hilton is photographed eating guacamole, you can talk about that. Perhaps if one of them was making a sour face, you could say that her expression would look better if she was eating Guac-n-Rock Guacamole. Topics of blogs are endless.

Bright Idea

Blogging allows you to reach your audience on a more personal level.

Blogging also allows you to share photos and external Web links with your readers. You can provide behind-the-scenes knowledge of how people act in the office each day. This will allow readers to connect with your business. It will also give future employees an idea of how things work at your company.

Blogging is a way to keep your consumers up-to-date on any

topic. Unlike your Web site content and the content of your advertisements, your blog's content will change often. This is a way to give your consumers new knowledge that would otherwise require a certain amount of lead time for other media.

Another reason to blog is to increase your business' name through search engine marketing. It is true that the more times your business' name comes up online, the more likely it is to be captured by the search engine crawlers and appear as a search result. This reason alone can help your company increase sales by drawing in more people than your competitors.

Content

Although blogs can be about anything, you need to find good content to keep your readers coming back to read more. One way to think about good content is by writing useful content for your readers. Useful content falls into one of the following categories:

- **Entertainment** — This is where your readers will find laughter and fun, light-hearted gossip. A popular entertainment blogger is Perez Hilton. You can visit his blog at **www.perezhilton.com.**

- **News** — This is where your readers will find updated information about news that is important to your company and to the reader.

- **Educational information** — This is where readers can be educated on a particular topic. For instance, Rock-n-Guac Guacamole may want to post a blog explaining how the guacamole is processed.

Two-Way Communication

Not only does a blog allow a way for you to communicate to your consumers, it also gives your consumers another way or reason to communicate with you. This is a valuable resource for many reasons. You can discover consumers' opinions on different products or their thoughts on new operations. This allows you to learn what they like or dislike in a matter of moments.

The market research that you can glean from consumer feedback can be astounding. It can help you cut back on costs for future research for your company. Though blogging feedback should not be generalized to a large audience, you can still use it to have a better idea of your market. Blogging feedback should not be used to forego other research.

If you have a large business, a blog can become an informal means of communicating with your employees. A blog will allow you, as an executive, to update employees on knowledge they may not otherwise know. A blog can take the average employees past the occasional newsletter and allow them to have a deeper knowledge of the business and how things are run. It should be noted, though, that if you are using your blog for this method, you may want to use it on your company's intranet rather than on the Internet.

Your company can use your blog to post different viewpoints from employees. You may want to monitor these posts, however, to make sure they do not give away valuable company information or secrets. Allowing your employees this means of communication gives readers a more diverse and inclusive look at how your business operates. It also shows your employees that you trust them to share their views with the rest of the world.

Tips for Writing a Good Blog

Although writing a good blog entry does not necessarily require the skills of a copywriter, it is possible to use one so that you are sure content is easy to read and grammatically correct.

Blog writing is the most informal of all Web writing. Here, you are not trying to sell anything. You are giving your readers content that they can use for knowledge, entertainment, or news. You do not need a flawless writing style. If your target market is teenagers, you may want to use "r" for "are" and "u" for "you." It will make you seem more personable and easier to relate to. However, if your target audience is baby boomers, you may not want to opt for "r"s and "u"s.

Have a great title. This is important to any blog or Web writing of any sort. The headline will allow the reader to easily see what the blog post is about and determine whether he or she wishes to read about that particular topic.

Repetition is another key for blogging. Repetition will help give your blog a steady rhythm and pace. It will also allow you more leverage at keeping certain key phrases in your readers' minds. Repetition becomes a way of persuasion. Repetition will allow search engines to pick up more on the words being repeated for better search engine results. Try repeating your company's name, for instance.

Make your blog post scannable. Most people are not going to sit and read your entire blog post. You want to make sure that certain key points are easy to scan. Options include writing in the inverted pyramid style, employing bullet points or lists, using section headers, and bolding or highlighting your text. These techniques will allow the reader to catch the most important parts of your blog, even if he or she does not read it entirely. Lists will almost always gain more visibility than the rest of your writing, so if you can put it in a list, do so.

Use images to add emphasis. Use an image only if it is something that is otherwise hard to describe in words. Make sure your image is clear and easy to see. The image should have a primary focal point and be interesting. You want to make sure that it is not grainy, blurry, or pixilated.

Include links to external information. Using these links can add greater value to your content because it can help validate your information. Make sure that the external link adds information you are otherwise unable to provide and that it is pertinent to your content. Also make sure that the links work properly. It is annoying to click on a link and then have it not work.

Bright Idea

Blogs can be an easy and fun way of communication. They are great for trying out new ideas and getting feedback from consumers.

List the date. Always be sure to date your blog post. This will allow readers to see when it was written and keep better track of newer information. This also allows you to go back and see where your business was a year in the past.

Give readers a way to contact you. This increases your two-way communication and allows readers to voice their ideas and opinions on your business and what you are writing about. Make sure that you have a "contact me at _____" phrase on the page or within the content of the blog. This will make it easier for readers.

How to Start Your Blog

If you already have a Web site, starting your blog is easy. Add another page to your Web site and begin using that page as your blog. Just update your blog when you want to, and keep the other posts displayed in a reverse chronological order. Have a link to the blog in other pages of your Web site so that readers can easily find it.

If you do not already have a Web site, getting a blog is still easy. You can sign up for a free blog at popular blogging Web sites, such as Blogger (**www.blogger.com**) or Word Press (**www.wordpress. com**). Choose your user name and password, and then start updating your blogs. Be sure to pick a professional name. You do not want to use "Hotgurl25" as your blogging name. It does not cast your business in a positive light. Think in terms of visibility and the amount of people who will be viewing your blog. They will not take you seriously if you have a name like that.

These blogs often have pre-made layouts that you can select from, making it even easier for you to communicate your message. You will not have to worry about any programming or design issues with your blog, and this ease will give you the ability to get to work quickly.

A disadvantage about using a pre-made blog from an outside site is that it does not lend as much credibility to your business. Using a blog on your own Web site is best because readers can find it more easily and will better associate it with your business.

However, if this is not an option, be sure to say your business' name in each post so that your consumer knows.

Social Networking

Other good places to start blogs and promote your business are on social networking Web sites, such as MySpace (**www.myspace. com**) and Facebook (**www.facebook.com**). These Web sites give you another way to increase your visibility among consumers and will also provide you with a means of reaching various target markets in a new way.

Signing up for these sites is free and easy. Register your name, and then you can set up your profile. Again, make sure to include your business' name and other information that you feel your consumers should know. Make sure to post links to your official Web site, if you have one.

Having profiles on these social networking sites will also increase your visibility in search engines. Your name will be stated more on various pages and will allow search engines more opportunity to pick it up.

You may find you need to update profiles and blogs less often than your official corporate blog. Or, you may have a different person communicate on these blogs and target them toward a different market. Or, you may choose to post the same blogs on each Web site.

These social networking sites enable people to leave comments. Therefore, you need to monitor these comments to make sure they reflect your business in a positive manner. You do not want a disgruntled customer leaving nasty comments for the world to see. If someone does leave a negative comment, try to contact them to make amends. However, you also have the opportunity to delete the negative comment. This can become a good venue for your consumers to communicate with each other and learn what other consumers think of your business. Be aware, though, that it can also work against you.

Summary

Having blogs helps increase your visibility among consumers and among search engines. It will allow you more opportunities to connect with your target audiences and spread the name of your business across the Web.

Because social networking sites offer free profiles to everyone, it is an advantage for your business to have a profile. This will give you a new space to connect with consumers and give you an opportunity to link the consumers to your corporate Web site.

Update your blogs as often as you want. Your content is up to you, but it should be informational or educational and written in an informal manner. If you are not updating your blogs often, at least monitor them on a regular basis.

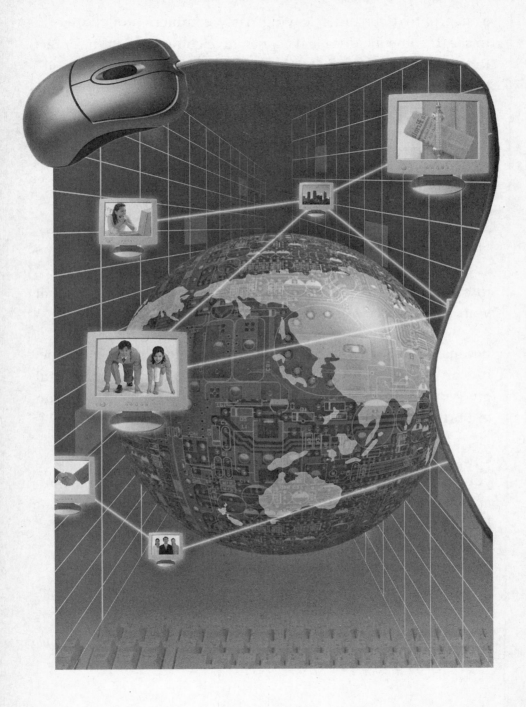

Reaching Your Target Market

"We target markets more than we target companies. We're in the business of targeting opportunities and adjusting our business to that."
Tom Skelton

With a plethora of Web sites available to advertise on, one may become overwhelmed with the choices available. Likewise, consumers may also become deeply saturated with the amount of products and services available to them. The ideal situation would be to achieve the most reach (who sees your ad) with as much frequency as possible (how many times those people see your ad) for as little money as possible. However, do not be led astray by Web sites that offer you advertising space for cheap; it is often not worth it.

Bright Idea

You have to know whom you are targetting to be effective in any advertising campaign.

Deciding where to advertise goes back to knowing who your target market is. It would not be effective for you to advertise on **myspace.com** when your target market never goes there. Likewise, it may cost more to advertise on **yahoo.com**, but if you know that 99 percent of your target market frequents **yahoo.com**, it may be cost-effective to advertise there. This being said, there is no perfect place to advertise online. You have to know who you want to target and then design a strategy that best finds and reaches that target market.

In 2007, **SearchEngineLand.com** put together a list of the top ten most visited Internet sites. They are as follows (**http:// searchengineland.com/070216-102423.php**):

1. Yahoo sites, 129 million

2. Time Warner Network, 117 million

3. Microsoft sites, 115 million

4. Google sites, 113 million

5. eBay, 81 million

6.   Fox Interactive Media, 75 million

7.   Amazon sites, 51 million

8.   Ask Network, 49 million

9.   Wikipedia sites, 43 million

10. New York Times Digital, 40 million

Four search engines, three news sites, one online encyclopedia, and two online shops make the list. By reviewing this list, you should see that if you are a small business, one of your best bets to promote your business would be contextual advertising through search engines, specifically Yahoo!, Google, MSN, and Ask. If you have not done so already, you might want to turn to eBay and Amazon to do business. And if you have a product or service that is truly noteworthy, you may want to have an article or be mentioned in Wikipedia.

What follows in this chapter are demographics that your business might choose to target and examples of popular Web sites that would be most effective at reaching them. You can find more specific demographic information on most of these sites by visiting them and clicking on the "Advertise With Us" link found near the bottom of the page. These Web sites may work well for your business to advertise on, or you may find that you should not advertise on any of them because of your target market or because of the price. All statistics were reported on the company's Web site in Febuary 2008 unless otherwise noted. Keep in mind that some of these statistics are constantly changing.

Everyone

If you have a broad target market, or if you are unclear on your target market, it may be best for you to use contextual advertising on a number of sites. The most popular search engines to use contextual advertising on are Google, Yahoo!, and MSN.

Since their main pages are not necessarily targeted toward any demographic, using these search engines may be a big help to your business. When you decide what key words best represent your product or service, you can begin targeting your target market on these search engines. Best of all, anyone who wants information is likely to turn to one of these search engines, making them a prime candidate for your advertising dollars.

Google

As of this writing, Google is the most popular search engine on the Internet. It is so popular that it has become a standard phrase for people to say, "Let me Google that," or ask, "Did you Google it?" With the amount of consumers using Google, it is a great choice for any advertiser to use to reach its consumer base through Google's popular contextual advertisements called Google AdWords. Google even makes it easy to keep track of your advertising on its Web site through the program called Google AdSense.

Google AdWords is a popular place for businesses to advertise their product or service. Google Adwords allows a business to invest as much or as little money into advertising as it wants. It also allows greater flexibility in the advertisement, because the business can always log into its account and change the text, and it is not obligated to advertise for a specific period.

If you have ever visited Google, you may have noticed the ads that appear as links, either at the top of the search results or on the right side. These advertisements appear because of what you searched for, and they are linked to certain words. Thus, Google AdWords allows you to cater your product or service to those people who are seriously interested in it. Google AdWords is providing a great service to consumers by allowing them an easier way to get the products that they want.

Yahoo!

Yahoo! is also a Web portal that people use to find information, second behind Google. However, Yahoo! also offers a variety of news and feature stories on its home page. Yahoo! has multiple subcategories of pages, where it offers information, and people can easily find these pages from direct links from the home page.

Like Google, Yahoo! offers text advertisements similar to AdWords. These advertisements operate in the same way, being based on targeted key word searches and offering about the same amount of text space as AdWords. The same advice applies to these Yahoo! text ads as to Google AdWords.

Unlike Google, Yahoo! offers an array of banner advertisements. Banner advertisements come by many names, which help clarify their position on the Web page. Yahoo! offers in-banner streaming for all its banner advertisements (see Chapter 11 for more on in-banner streaming).

Yahoo! offers businesses the ability to place their advertisement on its various pages. For example, Yahoo! has Web sites dedicated to entertainment, sports, dining, and more. Guac-n-Rock Guacamole may choose to advertise on one of Yahoo!'s food pages in an effort to reach people who shop for groceries or people who prepare food.

Though Yahoo! targets a mass audience at first glance, businesses can target their advertisements to certain demographics that visit Yahoo!'s subcategory pages. Yahoo! has put together a listing of where it ranks online in popular categories, such as search engine, e-mail, games, and music. Currently, according to Yahoo!, it is ranked in the top three in 23 of its key categories, and it is ranked number one in nine of those 23 categories.

MSN

Microsoft offers a search engine home page that is more akin to Yahoo!, because it offers the ability to search the Internet and offers news and feature stories to readers. Perhaps an added benefit to using MSN to advertise on is the fact that many computers have **msn.com** set as their default home page when they use Internet Explorer.

MSN also owns other Web pages that you can advertise on, and those pages have their target markets more narrowly defined.

Teenagers and Twenty-Somethings

The youth are often a difficult market for advertisers to reach. However, these young people are most familiar with the Internet and have grown up using it, making it a good media to reach this market.

Youth value convenience, and the Internet gives them that. They can easily make purchases online at the click of a button without ever leaving the comfort of their homes. This is great news if your business is mainly online.

Although members of this market may not have as much purchasing power as older generations, they are not hesitant to spend money. They are also more willing to make spur-of-the-moment purchases on their credit cards.

Members of this demographic also have a skeptical attitude toward advertising. They want to find out the facts about the products and services they are buying. They do not like being told what to do, which is another reason that this market is so difficult to reach. They value recommendations from their family and friends and those whom they trust. Members of this market like for products to be custom because they value individuality.

They like playing games online and taking quizzes. Women are more apt to enjoy these activities than men.

Some quick facts about the youth demographic:

- Not as hesitant as other demographics to spend money

- Technology-savvy

- Do not trust or like advertisements

- Value individuality

The following are Web sites that would be ideal at reaching this target market.

MySpace

MySpace is a social networking Web site that is often frequented by teenagers and twenty-somethings, though it is not unknown for the parents of these teenagers to have a MySpace account as well.

MySpace, being about social networking, allows you to reach members of this target audience and be their friend. A popular way to advertise on MySpace is to create your own MySpace profile for your business. This is free and will help your business in a variety of ways:

1. It provides exposure to a generation that is hard to reach.

2. It allows you to have free advertising.

3. It helps increase your search engine results because there is a new page that contains your business' name.

4. It gives you a way to connect to your consumers.

However, if you still want to place advertisements on MySpace, you can. Your business can advertise on MySpace's home page, which would come with a hefty price tag, or you can use banner advertisements on the pages within MySpace.

Facebook

Though originally designed for college students, Facebook started allowing anyone to have an account.

Businesses often do not use Facebook paid advertising because of the poor click-through rate; however, it may be an avenue your business wants to try because it is relatively inexpensive.

However, like MySpace, business can set up a free profile on Facebook. They can also create groups centered around their business and use this as a type of promotion.

YouTube

YouTube is a Web site devoted to displaying user videos. Anyone with an account can post a video and then decide who can view it. Videos on YouTube gain popularity through word of mouth. People tell other people that a video is great and pass it along. This can provide an excellent advertising opportunity for your company if you choose to create a video and then it is received well among viewers. Make sure it does not sound like an advertisement. You could try writing a script and having good product placement, much like a Webisode. Since you do not have to pay to post your video, it is inexpensive and cost-effective if you can use it to your advantage.

Companies such as Heinz Ketchup are using YouTube to create advertisements. These companies have hosted contests for consumers to create their next advertisement and place it on YouTube. Then other people can vote on the winner. This idea can play to your advantage to create buzz about your product; however, it also limits the control you have over your product's message.

You can also pay to have advertisements on YouTube. With an audience composed of 54 percent male and 46 percent female and more than 37 percent of users under the age of 34, this is a great place for your business to reach a younger demographic.

YouTube attracts 55 million unique users each month and has the eighth largest audience on the Internet.

Yahoo!

Members of this age group go to Yahoo! to get their news and entertainment. They also play Yahoo! Games, making these specific subcategories your business can use to reach this target age group.

Women

Women are good consumer targets for many businesses. They make more than 80 percent of the purchasing decisions in their homes, according to an article in Business Week titled "I Am Woman, Hear Me Shop," which you can find online at: **www.businessweek.com/bwdaily/dnflash/feb2005/nf20050214_9413_db_082.htm**. This article says that women are less likely to be influenced by negative advertisements and are more likely to research a product before they buy it. This means that women consumers are going online to find information about these products and services before they make a purchase.

Women are often considered more sensitive and caring, and they like advertisements that appeal to their nurturing side. They care about their health and about the health and well-being of their families. Since women are so concerned about health issues, cause marketing plays a special role for them. Women will notice the healthy heart symbol, the going red symbol, or the breast cancer awareness ribbon.

Women often need to be in multiple places throughout their day, whether that be work and school for their children, baseball practice, or a parent-teacher association (PTA) meeting. Thus, their lives are increasingly becoming more on-the-go. Convenience is a trend that matters to women everywhere. They like quick and easy products and services that address their needs.

When targeting women, your business should make sure to get the little stuff right. Women focus on the details of advertisements and Web sites. They pay attention to the words and the designs. They also pay attention to the service and how their needs are met. When trying to target women, remember to sweat the details.

Some quick facts about women as a demographic:

- Have the most buying power

- Will research a product before buying

- Strong believers in cause marketing

- Lead busy lives

The following sections include some typical Web sites where you can reach women.

iVillage.com

iVillage is a hub for specialized women's information. Women visit iVillage to learn information about a variety of topics that they find important, such as fashion, dieting, pregnancy, and more.

Businesses can purchase banner ads on iVillage.

Cosmopolitan

It is no surprise that women like to read magazines and that their interest extends online. Cosmopolitan (**www.cosmopolitan.com**) is a favorite magazine of women.

It offers women advice and knowledge of all sorts but especially pertaining to sex. Women who read this magazine trust the experts providing the advice. They also find the stories interesting and appealing to their needs.

Cosmopolitan is owned by Hearst Digital Media, which also owns and controls the Web site advertising for several other related sites, including CosmoGIRL, Country Living, Marie Claire, Redbook, TEEN, and Seventeen. Together, the sites have more than 7.1 million unique users per month, making them a great place to reach women. However, advertising on these Web sites will often come with a higher price tag.

Oprah.com

Women everywhere tune in to Oprah on their television sets daily. It is no surprise that when they go online, they are also tuning into Oprah on their computers.

Oprah.com provides compelling feature stories and advice for women's everyday lives. The Web site also provides updates on upcoming show events and contests. Women trust Oprah, and her opinions do matter. Thus, Oprah's esteem may carry through to the advertisements found on her Web site. Again, these advertisements may come with a hefty price tag and may be possible only with a large advertising budget.

myLifetime.com

Another popular destination for women online is **mylifetime. com**. This Web site is the online portal for the Lifetime television station. Here, women can get updated on current celebrity gossip and the upcoming schedule for the station. They can also take part in an online community and play games.

Lifetime has 3.7 million unique visitors per month, with 33.5 million monthly page views. Their strongest demographic is females aged 35 to 54.

MSN Women

MSN offers a portal specifically for women at **women.msn.com**. This Web site is centered on a woman's needs and includes feature stories, an online community, advice columnists, recipes, health advice, and Hollywood gossip.

The advantage to advertising on MSN as opposed to more popular women's Web sites is that it can be more affordable for small businesses, and it still provides the opportunity to reach the target market.

Health Web Sites

Women are concerned about their health and the health of their families. They often will visit Web sites such as **Webmd.com**, **womenfitness.net**, and **healthywomen.org** to find solutions to their questions about their health and advice on how to stay healthy. If your business offers a product or service that relates to health in any way, these Web sites could be the perfect venue you need to reach health-conscious women.

Men

Men tend to make judgments based on their first impressions. They often know what they want, and they buy it. Unlike women, men do not feel the need to deeply research a product before making a purchase.

With men, sex sells. Look at most advertisements targeted to men. These advertisements either contain an alluring woman or provide a unique advantage to using a product, often in an attempt to make the man attract a woman. This does not mean you need to put a picture of a naked woman on your advertisement. You can gain the attention of male consumers by being clever and using humor or even alluding to sex without showing or saying anything sexual.

Men tend to visit the following types of Web sites: tech blogs, sports, news, games, and men's magazines.

Some quick facts about men as a demographic:

- Make quick judgments

- Sex sells

- Enjoy sports and technology

Guyville.com

Men like technology and always want to learn about the latest products. Web sites such as **guyville.com** are dedicated to showing men the newest technology.

Guyville.com is listed as the second most frequented Web site by men on **toptensites.com**, coming in behind *Maxim* magazine.

Advertisements on smaller sites will be cheaper than well-known Web sites, which is an advantage to a small business.

ESPN.com and Sports Illustrated.com

It is not news that men like sports, making ESPN and Sports Illustrated sites a great place to reach them. Guys like to get the latest updates on sports scores and new events in the world of sports. However, because these two sites are often frequented, advertising on them will likely come at a large price.

ESPN.com is where guys go to check the latest sports scores and news. The median age of men on this site is 30, and 73 percent of those men are employed full-time with an average household income of $77,000.

Sports Illustrated (**http://sportsillustrated.cnn.com**) is where men go to read about sports and sports news. This site reaches a weekly audience of almost 21 million adults. The highest target market of visitors to *Sports Illustrated* is males with a median age of 40 and a median household income of $84,000.

News Sites

Men like to keep up with news and politics, making it beneficial for your company to reach them on news sites such as **cnn.com**, **foxnews.com**, or your local newspaper's Web site.

Cnn.com has 28.4 million average monthly unique visitors to its site, with a median age of 44.7 and a median household income of about $76,000. Visitors often spend about 30 minutes while there.

Foxnews.com has 8.5 million unique visitors per month. With a median age of 47 and a median household income of $73,000, these users are predominantly males (60 percent) and spend about 49 minutes on the Web site.

Once again, however, these sites will come with a higher price tag that smaller businesses may not be able to afford. This is why a good local option may be your newspaper's Web site or a newspaper in nearby city's Web site. The expense for these Web sites is often smaller, and it is a good way to reach a local audience. If you contact the newspaper, ask it for the demographic information to see if it caters to your target market.

Gaming Web Sites

Men like to play games online, and they also like to find out about the games that they play offline. Men visit these sites to find out about upcoming game releases and to find out cheats to games they are currently playing.

IGN.com is a popular gaming Web site where men can find out news and cheats for their games. IGN has 35 million unique users per month, with a core visitor base of 18- to 35-year-old males. This site is part of a network of Web sites, including **rottentomatoes. com**, **askmen.com**, and **gamespy.com**, creating more integrated ways for your business to advertise.

Gamespot.com is a popular place for men to play games and find cheats online. Gamespot attracts and retains one of the Web's largest concentrations of 13- to 34-year-old males. With 140 million unique visitors to the Web site per month, 97 percent are male, with an average age of 24. The Web site describes its users as loyal, diverse, and influential.

Yahoo! Games is another popular place to reach male gamers, especially if you are already advertising with Yahoo!.

Men's Magazines

Men also like to keep up with popular trends and get advice from their favorite magazines. This carries over onto the Internet, too.

Maxim (**www.maxim.com**) is the most visited Web site by men according to **toptensites.com**. *Maxim* offers men news, sex advice, gossip, and photos. *Maxim* is also in a network with two other magazines, *Blender* and *Stuff*, which are also often read by men.

Maxim is so heavily frequented that it is no surprise that it comes with a higher price tag than other Web sites targeting males.

Men visit *GQ* Magazine's Web site, **www.gq.com**, to find new style and news information. This Web site boasts a median age of 34, with an average household income of about $80,000. More than 71 percent of consumers visiting the Web site are men.

African-Americans

African-Americans have been represented in advertising in the mass media only since the mid-1960s. However, with a population exceeding 34 million in the United States, they are not to be overlooked as consumers.

African-Americans have a tendency to value togetherness, and they take pride in their heritage. They tend to define their own style rather than going with what society dictates. Family and religion are important values to African-Americans.

African-Americans tend to spend their money on status symbols, such as cars, electronics, and jewelry, making these good markets for targeting them. However, upscale African-Americans tend to purchase generic equivalents and private-label goods, while poorer African-Americans buy national brands.

Some quick facts about the African-American demographic:

- They spend more than average on personal care, such as hair styling, manicures, and massages, for men and women.

- They spend more than average on hosiery, women's accessories, home electronics, and jewelry.

- They will pay more to get "the best" possible.

- They tend to adopt styles that are not part of the mainstream.

Web sites that target African-Americans:

Blackplanet.com

Black Planet tops the list of **Blackwebportal.com**'s 30 most popular Web sites among African-Americans. Black Planet has 16.5 million members, with 80 million unique page views per month. Black Planet is a Web site dedicated to issues pertaining to the African-American culture and provides advice from popular

African-American celebrities, such as Kimora Lee Simmons and Mo'Nique. Black Planet is also a social networking site exclusively devoted to the African-American community. It is the fifth most-trafficked social networking Web site, behind the popular MySpace and Facebook.

Bet.com

Black Entertainment Television is a popular place to reach African-Americans, and that popularity carries over to the Internet. At **Bet.com**, consumers can find the most up-to-date information about African-American music and entertainment and also find out what is new with the television station.

Vibe.com

Vibe.com is the online version of *Vibe Magazine*. Like the magazine, **Vibe.com** is dedicated to bringing consumers the latest information and news related to hip-hop and urban life.

Vibe.com has 1.5 million unique visitors monthly. The median age for the site is 28. The male-to-female ratio for the site is 58 percent male to 42 percent female. **Vibe.com** boasts that by advertising on its site, your business is nine times more likely to reach African-Americans online.

Essence.com

Essence.com is the online version of *Essence Magazine*. It is a leading Web site to reach African-American women. *Essence* offers the latest fashion trends, advice, and news. The average *Essence* consumer is female (96 percent), 38 years old, and making roughly $46,000 a year.

Hispanics

The Hispanic market is rapidly growing in the United States and is expected to become the largest minority group in the United States in 2010. Due to this growth, Hispanic buying power is projected to increase from 11 percent to 14 percent by 2010.

There is no consensus on the identifying characteristics of what makes someone Hispanic. People belonging to this group have many names for themselves, including Latino, Mexican, Mexican-American, Puerto Rican, Cuban, and "Other." Keep in mind that each of these groups have different distinguishing characteristics and many dislike being referred to as a member of a different type of Hispanic group.

Bright Idea

Everyone is unique. Do not think just because groups have one similarity that they are entirely similiar.

Hispanics tend to have higher birthrates and larger families than the average American, and their household income is less. They place emphasis on family and children. Like African-Americans, Hispanics care about preserving their culture and traditions. They also want to preserve their language, with many of them speaking Spanish in their homes. They tend to be big fans of sports, namely soccer, baseball, and boxing.

Some quick tips to advertise to the Hispanic demographic:

- Do not use any negative stereotypes.

- Do not refer to every Hispanic as a "Mexican."

- If you decide to advertise in Spanish, realize that different words have different meanings among different Hispanic groups.

- Try out your advertisement on someone who considers himself or herself Hispanic before launching it.

- Young Hispanics are driving the online market.

- Most mainstream Web sites, such as AOL, MSN, Yahoo!, and CNN, have Web portals dedicated to the Hispanic market.

MiGente.com

Migente.com is an English-language site dedicated to the Hispanic community, aimed at the second-generation immigrant who speaks English as his or her primary language. The Web site has 2.8 million users that come from a variety of Hispanic backgrounds. The Web site is host to music, style, and news that is popular among the Hispanic culture. It is also provides social networking among Hispanics.

Latino.aol.com

America Online Latino offers Hispanics a Spanish version of the popular Web site. Here, all articles and advertisements are in Spanish. The articles cater to the Hispanic community and showcase issues important to Latin culture. AOL offers different advertising programs that can easily be designed to meet your business' needs. You can choose what time of day to advertise, the geography of the people browsing, different ad formats, and more.

Terra.com

Terra.com is a global informational Web portal dedicated to the Hispanic community. The Terra network operates some of the most popular Hispanic Web sites in the United States and Latin America. **Terra.com** has more than 45 million unique visitors per month. It provides coverage of popular Hispanic news, sports, music, and entertainment.

Asian-Americans

Asian-Americans are also a rapidly growing ethnic group. This group tends to be the most affluent and highly educated. Like the Hispanic market, many diverse people call themselves Asian-Americans; however, unlike the Hispanic market, these people do not share a common language or culture.

There are six distinct Asian markets:

1. Chinese

2. Koreans

3. Vietnamese

4. Filipinos

5. Japanese

6. Asian Indians

Since the Asian-American subculture is so diverse, advertisers in the United States have found it hard to reach this demographic. Although many of the most popular sites online, such as Yahoo!,

AOL, and MSN, offer specialty pages to many demographics, Asian-Americans are not often one of them.

Although Asian-Americans have many differences, these groups do have a few things in common. Asians value group harmony and family togetherness. They identify with other Asians and place a high value on educating their children.

Some quick facts about the Asian-American demographic:

- They are often motivated to save money and invest it.

- They tend to spend more money on education.

- According to Biz Report (**www.bizreport.com/2007/05/90_ percent_of_asian_americans_go_online.html**), 90 percent of Asian-Americans go online.

www.AsianAve.com

Owned by the same company as Black Planet and MiGente, Asian Ave is one of the premier online destinations for Asian-Americans. This Web site is designed to be a Web portal that delivers information about news, fashion, and trends important to the Asian-American subculture. It is also a social networking site devoted to Asian-Americans.

Gay/Lesbian/Bisexual/Transgender (GLBT)

The gay, lesbian, bisexual, and transgender subculture (GLBT) began gaining popularity in the 1990s. Marketers have since begun recognizing this subculture and targeting it.

Members of the GLBT subculture places a strong emphasis on the value of friendships. They are more apt to interact with friends who share the same sexual orientation. Often, they are politically active and aware of current and social issues.

The best way to target people in this group is to be accepting to their life style. They are especially receptive to companies that are accepting of them, even if they are not completely satisfied with that company's products or services. Members of this group will easily become brand-loyal and promote to their friends brands that recognize their needs. They will specifically avoid and boycott companies that they find homophobic.

The 2000 United States Census determined that one in nine couples is a same-sex couple, and 22 percent of male partners and 34 percent of female partners reported having children. Weddings among same-sex couples are gaining popularity, and many companies are beginning, if they have not already, to offer benefits to domestic partners.

Some quick facts about the GLBT demographic:

- They place a strong value on friendships.

- They are brand-loyal to companies that are accepting of their life style.

- They are involved in current and social issues.

Glee.com

Glee.com became one of the top 20 gay Web sites within five months of launching in early 2007. It provides news and entertainment of interest to the gay community. It is also one of the only social and professional networking Web sites for the gay community.

Planetout.com

Planetout.com is a Web portal for the gay community, offering news, feature stories, and links of interest. It also provides a singles dating site and links to competitions specifically designed for the gay community. Planet Out has an audience composed mainly of men (85 percent) between 18 and 34. The Web site receives 500,000 unique viewers per month.

Gay.com

Gay.com is another Web portal for the gay community. This Web site offers headlines, personals, local information, and chat rooms for the gay community. Owned by Planet Out, it also captures an audience of about 85 percent men between 18 and 34. However, this Web site has more than 3,700,000 unique visitors per month.

Out.com

Out.com is the online extension of *Out Magazine*. This magazine is devoted to gay readers, bringing them feature stories, dating advice, fashion advice, and gossip. Out's demographic is composed of 72 percent males, aged 35 to 44, with an average household income of $119,000.

Summary

You can target many different subcultures in the United States. Choosing a subculture that is not mainstream may prove to be less expensive in advertising expenditures and give you a targeted campaign so that you can easily measure its effectiveness.

Although finding research for your target market may prove a costly investment, you can always find information by visiting the Web sites you are looking into and viewing their press releases. Most Web sites have downloadable PDF press kits available to you under the section "Advertise with Us." Reading these press kits can give you information about that particular Web site and also about the target market you are searching for. So even if you are not thinking about advertising on *Vogue*'s Web site because it is out of your budget, reading its press kit may give you a keen insight into your target market without you having to spend any money.

If you are targeting a local market, try advertising through your newspaper's Web site or a local radio station's Web site. These sites can prove to be a good investment for your company and are less expensive than large names. They can help you target a specific region and get a localized response.

Another way to gain publicity online is to register through your local chamber of commerce. Even if this gives you only a small mention on its Web page, it will allow you to show that you are a member and prove to your consumers that you have a legitimate business. The more times you get your business' name mentioned on the Internet, the better it will be for you.

Designing 101 for Copywriters

"Designers can create normalcy out of chaos; they can clearly communicate ideas through the organizing and manipulating of words and pictures."
Jeffery Veen

As a copywriter, you might never need to be concerned with design. You will just be instructed to write attention-grabbing copy. The art is left to the art director or designer to come up with. It is the designer who is responsible for determining color schemes, typography, photos, and any visual element in the advertisement. However, if you are working in a small company, you may end up becoming the copywriter and the art director; therefore, it is important for you to be acquainted with the elements of design so that you can create a stunning advertisement without knowing too much about art.

Bright Idea

Having a basic understanding of design will help you communicate with the designer more effectively to ensure a quality advertisement.

The Rough

It is always helpful to create a rough sketch of what you want to do with an advertisement. This sketch should show where you intend to place the copy and the visuals. Even if you are working with an art director, it is beneficial to create a rough so that you can convey what you are envisioning.

First things first: You do not have to know how to draw. All you need to do is write your headline where you want it to appear and draw boxes for your other elements. Often, a box with an X through it indicates a photo or other visual element. You may find it beneficial to have a description of what you want the visual element to be so that you can better communicate the idea to the art director or to your employer. This will allow others to know what you are envisioning. Copywriters have a knack for writing about how they see things, whereas art directors have a knack for showing how they see things.

Roughs are often drawn on paper. You can create several different roughs to generate different ideas based on the same headline.

This will help build your creativity and show you different solutions for the problem at hand.

A good idea is to take the rough that you like and set up a template for it on your computer. You do not need any other program other than a basic word processor, such as Microsoft Word, to do this. Just re-create your drawing in a neater fashion. Then save these templates for a later use. This will allow you to quickly find a template and fit your copy in it for the future. You may have several different templates that you keep, such as ones for Web sites, skyscrapers, towers, and classifieds.

The Uses of Color

Color can lead people to do many things. For instance, painting a dining room red causes people to consume more food, which is why this is a popular choice in restaurants. Color can also give people a sense of emotion. For instance, green is often perceived as a calming color. However, colors can have dual meanings. For example, blue can mean calm and serene, but it can also mean cold and icy.

The following is a list of popular colors and their subjective meanings. Think of them in terms of your copy message. If you want people to feel a certain way, you may decide to use a certain color to help enhance the mood.

Red: Red is one of the primary colors. It is often perceived as promoting violence and aggression because it is bold and assertive and the color of blood. In warfare, blood can be seen as the drawing of power from the weak to the strong. Red can also be seen as the color of love and passion. Gifts of red roses signify love each Valentine's Day. When red is used in conjunction with green, it can make people think of Christmas. An important thing to remember when using the color red is that it is one color that is particularly difficult for color-blind people to distinguish.

Pink: Pink is often seen as a feminine color and often used to represent baby girls. Many men find pink to be a weak color and do not like associating with it. Used on products, it can convey breast cancer awareness. Pink also can be seen as a flirtatious color.

Orange: Orange is a color that does not have many meanings. It is a warm color and often thought of as fire. It brings about a feeling of cheerfulness and festivities. Bright orange is often associated with hunting. Orange can become overbearing if used too much.

Yellow: Most people think of the sun when they think of the color yellow. It is bright and tends to elicit feelings of happiness and warmth. However, yellow has also become known as a color of cowardice, such as in the phrase, "yellow-bellied." Yellow can be harsh on the eyes in its purest form. It should be used sparingly and with caution.

Green: Green is calming and found everywhere in nature. Since green is considered a cool color, it recedes when placed with brighter hues. Green also has a negative connotation because it can mean that someone is inexperienced or a novice. Green can also mean "sickly," such as "green around the gills." Green offers a variety of shades to pick from. However, green is also another color that is hard for color-blind people to easily distinguish.

Blue: Blue is often used as a peaceful and soothing color. It can remind people of the sky or the sea. Banks often use blue in their logos because of the calming, peaceful effect this recessive color has. Blue also has other connotations, though, such as someone being in a "blue mood," meaning that he or she is sad. Blue can be thought of as "icy" and "cold," especially when mixed with white, which is also a cool color.

Purple: Purple is associated with royalty and wealth. It is believed to be a color of good judgment and is a good color to be used for meditation. A combination of the warmest and coolest colors (red and blue), purple is sometimes believed to be the "ideal" color. This color often is favored among children.

Black: Black is one of the easiest colors to read, especially when paired with a white background. However, black is thought of as depressing by most people. It is associated with death or violence. Black can also be thought of as sexy and alluring, hence why women often choose the "little black dress."

White: White is often thought of as the color of purity and innocence in the Western culture. In China, however, white is associated with mourning.

Color Combinations

There are several different color combinations to choose from, and entire books have been devoted to color theory alone. First, we will discuss the most basic two-color pairings with regard to a solid-color text on a solid-color background.

The basic colors fit into one of two categories: warm and cool. Cool colors — blue, purple, green — will recede. Warm colors — red, yellow, orange — will progress. This means that if you use these colors together, the cooler of the colors will have a tendency to fade into the background while the warmer colors will stand out. Put items that you want to stand out in the warmer colors so that they will become more prominent in the viewer's mind.

A good trick of the trade is to use black text on a white background when possible. This is the easiest pattern for anyone to read. If you want to call attention to something, you can reverse this pattern by putting white text on a black background. However, it will slow the reader down. It will also become burdensome and costly for people to print if they want to print out your information.

Bright Idea

Be careful when using red and green. Color-blind people find these two colors hard to distinguish.

If you decide not to use black text on white, you should realize that it is easiest to match a dark color with a light color for better readability. It is better to put the lighter color as the background and the darker color as the text. Following are some examples of good and bad color combinations:

Good color combinations:

- black and white

- red and white

- blue and white

- yellow and dark blue

- dark green and white

- yellow and black

- light blue and dark blue

- light blue and black

- purple and white

Bad color combinations:

- black and red

- green and red

- yellow and red

- blue and red

- yellow and white

- orange and white

- orange and yellow

- green and blue

- black and blue

Another important note about color: Try not to mix green and red together, especially if you need each of the colors to be discerned separately. These two colors are the least distinguishable by color-blind people, which may make it difficult for them to read your Web site.

Other color combinations that work:

- **Primary colors** — red, yellow, and blue

- **Secondary colors** — purple, green, and orange

- **Warm colors** — red, yellow, and orange

- **Cool colors** — purple, blue, and green

Color is an important part of any design. If you are unsure of the colors you choose, you may want to get a second opinion. You can, of course, combine more than two colors together in any design; just make sure your design is easy to read and understand. There is nothing worse than getting your colors wrong and making people not want to look at your advertisement or Web site.

CMYK vs. RGB

Although you may never need to know the difference between CMYK and RGB, it can be beneficial when communicating with a designer.

CMYK stands for cyan, magenta, yellow, and black. This is the type of process colors that are used in print. When you open up a magazine or newspaper, what you are seeing are combinations of different-colored dots. If you look through a loupe magnifier, you can easily distinguish the various dots, though they are not often visible to the naked eye.

RGB stands for red, green, and blue. This is the type of color process that is used in electronics and what you will be using on the Web.

Though the two colors that you pick may seem the same in their end result, there are variations. It is best to create your advertisement and design in whichever color set you will ultimately be using so that you can accurately see the end result.

Typography

Another key element in making sure people can read your text is the font that your text is in. Just because you can read the text on your computer does not necessarily mean that others can read the text on their computer.

Type can be split into many categories, but for simplicity's sake, we will divide them into two main categories: serif and sans serif. The main difference between these fonts may seem subtle, but it affects readability more than you might think. Serif fonts are fonts, such as this one, that have tiny features at the end of the strokes within the letter. An example is that this book is written in a serif font (Book Antiqua). Sans serif fonts, such as the font used for the Case Studies in this book, are fonts that do not have these strokes within the letter. The following is an example of a serif and sans serif font (the letter on the left is a serif font).

A A

Serif fonts are often easier for people to read. The serifs help connect the letters and make people read faster. Thus, these typefaces are good to have for long blocks of text. Sans serif fonts, on the other hand, cause people to slow down in their reading. Thus, these fonts are good to use for titles and headers to break up text and make the reader slow down.

Popular Serif Fonts

- Times New Roman (Times New Roman)

- Garamond (Adobe Garamond)

- Courier (Courier)

Popular Sans Serif Fonts

- Arial (Arial)

- Univers (Univers)

- Helvetica (Helvetica)

Serif fonts are easier for people to read and sans serif fonts slow readers down.

It is best to use a typeface that most people have on their computer to decrease any compatibility issues you may have. This is more important for your Web site text than for any advertisement, because ads are graphics that have the font already embedded in them. Web sites, on the other hand, may not always have the fonts embedded in them, which will create difficulty for a reader who does not have that font, and it may cause your Web site to look different from what you intend. Readers will see the standard font that their computer reverts to. If you are importing a graphic that contains type for your Web site, font compatibility is not an issue.

It is best to use any standard Windows font for your Web site, since most people use Windows as their operating system. The fonts listed previously are good standard choices for your Web site.

Though it may be tempting, try to avoid novelty fonts, especially in your Web site text. These fonts can be difficult for people to read and sometimes overbearing. Be careful if you choose these for your advertisements as well, for the same reasons.

You also want to limit the number of different types of fonts that you use. On a large-scale project, you may want to keep it to three different fonts. For smaller-scale projects, you might want to keep it to two. If you use a serif font for a headline, you might want to use a sans serif font for the subheadlines or vice versa.

Not all fonts look good together. You can make sure you have fonts that match by using the same font face in regular type and also in italic or bold type. Fonts of the same family always go together and look good.

Bright Idea

If your text is contained in a flattened image, search engines will not be able to read it for keywords.

Leading, Tracking, and Kerning

Leading deals with the amount of space vertically between lines. The more vertical space you have, the easier it is to read the type. Think of it in terms of increasing paragraphs to double spacing in Microsoft Word. This makes the text easier to read.

An example is that this book is done with a 17-point leading.

I can increase my leading between sentences to make it easier

to read; however, if I increase it too much, it will become more

difficult to read, like this paragraph.

Likewise, I can condense my leading and make it more difficult
to read because there is not enough space between the sentences,
like in this paragraph.

You should have a greater leading when working with sans serif fonts than you would when working with serif fonts. Sans serif fonts slow the reader down, so you need to make readability easier.

The leading should be at least 120 percent of your type size. For example, if you use a 12-point font, your leading should be at least 14.4. This would be the standard automatic setting in design programs such as Adobe InDesign. You can always increase your leading for greater legibility. If you are unfamiliar with design programs, a good example of adjusting the spacing between your sentences is when you use double spacing in a Microsoft Word document. Double-spaced documents are easier to read and sift through than single-spaced documents.

Tracking deals with the amount of space horizontally between letters. You do not want too much or too little kerning. It is best not to adjust kerning in your body copy. The only time you might want to kern your letters is if you find a line of type that runs together. You can increase your kerning to space out the words. Kerning is often used for letters in larger type for headlines and subheadlines.

Ideally, you do not want to kern your letters, especially in body copy. If you kern them too close, then they will look like this paragraph.

Likewise, if you kern them too far apart, they will start to look like this paragraph.

Kerning pertains to the amount of space between the individual letters. You probably will not have to deal with much kerning. It is mostly used on the large type found in headlines and subheads in advertisements to make sure everything looks perfect.

Photography and Art

Advertisements and Web sites likely incorporate some type of artwork. This may comprise the bulk of the piece, or it may be minimal.

Art should always serve a purpose. It may be showcasing a product or illustrating a point. Art should never be placed in an advertisement or on a Web site just to fill space. Make the art relevant and interesting.

If you are starting out in your business, you may not be able to afford a professional photographer for a photo shoot of your product. If you shoot your own art, make sure your artwork is clear and focused. You do not want to place grainy or pixilated art in an advertisement. It makes you look unprofessional.

With any kind of artwork, you may want it 300 dpi and in CMYK for print. However, for Web, you can have the artwork be 72 dpi, and it should be in RGB. The difference here is because saving a photo at a higher resolution will take a long time to load. Also, monitors show color in light, or RGB, whereas printers print in process colors, or CMYK. Though there is not a large difference between the two color formats, subtle differences will occur.

Another difference between print and Web is what file format you can save your photographs in. The most acceptable file format for the Web is JPEG, but you will never want to use a JPEG for print materials. JPEGs will flatten your images and reduce their size. This will cause the images to load faster. Anyone using a computer will also be able to download JPEGs and be able to open them. Other acceptable file formats for the Web include PNG and GIF.

Summary

Though you may never have a need to know about design, it is good to have a basic understanding in order to communicate with a designer more effectively Also realize that the design will play a major role in the look and feel of an advertisement.

Case Study: Nigel Fletcher

What made you want to become a copywriter?

As a child, I used to love the double-page spread ads in the Sunday color supplements, which seemed so clever, like minor works of art. That was what I wanted to do because I knew I was good at thinking in both words and pictures.

What was your first assignment? How did you feel about it?

My first job was writing a tiny ad for a Volvo dealership in the north of England. I felt more confident about it than I should have.

What do you know now that you wish you had known when you first started?

I wish I had realized that the only purpose of an ad is to sell a product or make people think well of a company.

What is the toughest copywriting challenge you faced?

Writing a brochure selling the benefits of investing in metal futures on the London Stock Exchange. Forward trading was as mysterious as the black arts to me then … and still is.

How does Web copywriting differ from traditional copywriting?

Most people visit Web sites purely for information and are in a hurry. Too much marketing-style content can be counterproductive.

Who are some of the clients you have worked for?

Audi, Cadbury, Ciba-Geigy, Hyundai, Minolta, Poggenpohl Kitchens, Seiko, Vodaphone, Premier Percussion.

What is your biggest success? What copy have you crafted that you loved?

To me, the real skill in copywriting is writing headlines that work dynamically with pictures. One of my most successful ads was for a company offering personal loans that just had a picture of a bottle of shark repellent. This brought in millions of dollars in business.

What are the best tips you have for successful Web copywriting?

The same as for any kind of copywriting — put yourself in the position of the person

Case Study: Nigel Fletcher

reading the copy. Get rid of anything that is not relevant or is just indulgent word play.

Do you feel it is more important in copywriting to be creative or a salesperson?

In copywriting, they should work together dynamically every time.

What part of the Web do you find it easiest and hardest to write for (Web sites, banner ads, or e-mail) and why?

Every job is hard — if it is not, you are not giving it enough attention.

How do you succeed in writing Web copy?

With Web sites, keep it clear, break things up into short paragraphs or bullet points, think about the navigation structure, give respect to search engine optimization, and ensure that a visit to the Web site is as easy and rewarding as possible. For banner ads and so on, get noticed. Give a reason to click through.

What makes the Internet a great media for advertising?

People often come to a site because they are already interested in the product area or service, so you have a head start.

Which companies do you feel do best advertising on the Internet?

Online retailers can do great if they find the right specialized niche. The usual mistake is to try and rival the big, established Web-based companies. If you can sell a better mousetrap ....

Advertising Copywriter

Birmingham, U.K.

www.wordstorm.co.uk

Section 3

Where to Go From Here

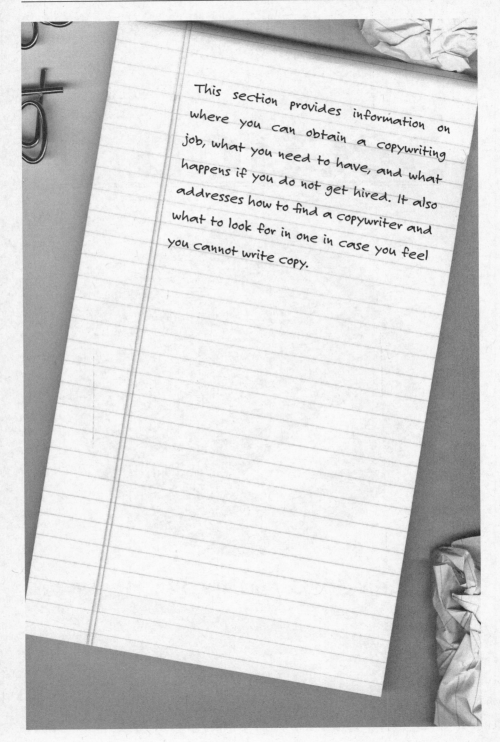

This section provides information on where you can obtain a copywriting job, what you need to have, and what happens if you do not get hired. It also addresses how to find a copywriter and what to look for in one in case you feel you cannot write copy.

What to Look for in a Copywriter

"If you think hiring professionals is expensive, try hiring amateurs."
Anonymous

Perhaps you have decided that writing Web copy is not for you. That is all right. Before you hire someone else to do it for you, it is best to know the basic principles of copywriting, which you should have gleaned from this book. You also need to know what to look for when you hire someone.

Freelance

You can find freelance writers from various Web sites. Popular ones include:

- elance.com

- guru.com

- odesk.com

- journalismjobs.com

Here you can set the price for your project and allow freelance writers to place their bids on how much they are willing to accept for the project. It is simple to set up an account, and you can get started right away.

Begin hiring your Web copywriter by first checking his or her credentials. Though a résumé does not necessarily provide an accurate description of a person's work, you can bet that if this person worked for a Fortune 100 company as a copywriter, he or she is good. However, if a person does not have much experience, that does not necessarily mean he or she will be bad.

Bright Idea

Good writers cost good money. Do not hire a copywriter becomes one places a bid so low that it is almost too good to be true.

Students and young professionals are on these sites, as are as seasoned veterans. You can often hire less-experienced people for less money than you would pay someone with experience.

This could become a win-win situation for your company and the other person. You gain quality work for an inexpensive price, and this person gains experience for his or her résumé and a piece for his or her portfolio. This option is good if you have a limited budget.

After you check the résumé, check the portfolio. The sites previously mentioned allow people to post their work online. Take the opportunity to read samples of their copywriting before hiring them.

These samples are a good indication of their talent. If someone is lacking grammatical skills or does not write well, you may want to pass on hiring this person. The writing you see is likely what you are going to get for your own Web copywriting needs.

Bright Idea

Knowing how to write good copy is an asset in hiring a good copywriter.

The last thing you want to look at is a person's rating. Many sites allow employees to leave feedback. This feedback tells you how dedicated a worker the person is before you hire him or her. If someone constantly has the same information written about him or her (good or bad), it is a good indication of what to expect when this person works for you.

When looking for a Web copywriter, you might consider finding someone who can also design or proofread your Web site, if you do not possess these skills. This will enable you to get a complete package and the most for your money.

One advantage of hiring someone on a freelance basis is that you can always choose not to use him or her again if you do not like the produced work. It also allows your business not to have to produce consistent work for an employee.

Full-Time

Your business may require regular copywriting, in which case you may find yourself needing to fill the position with a full-time, in-house employee. This is a good option for your business if your business's needs grow in excess of what you can pay individual freelancers.

The advantage of hiring someone in-house is that you can set the hourly rate or salary. This will allow you to better budget your business' needs and also provide someone with steady work. If the work becomes too much for one person to bear, you can either hire another person or bring in a freelancer to share the burden.

Another advantage of having someone in-house is that your work will be consistent. The employee will be able to develop a style based on your preferences and incorporate that into all your business's materials. Having multiple individuals working on various projects does not give your business the consistency that one or two full-time employees can provide.

Hiring a full-time employee is much the same as hiring a freelancer. You need to look at the person's portfolio and evaluate his or her résumé. You can check with previous employers or references to better evaluate the quality of the applicant's work. Also, you will be able to get a good gauge of the applicant's personality in the interview to see how he or she will fit into your work environment.

Summary

Hiring someone can, and will, always be a tricky task. You need to find someone who meshes well with your business and provides consistent, quality work. If you hire someone and do not like his or her work, do not be afraid to tell this person or provide constructive criticism. Your business has a right to have good work that is of a quality you like. Likewise, if you dislike the work provided, the copywriter has a right to know why and how to improve his or her work in the future — if not for your business, then for his or her next endeavor.

Case Study: Lisa Banks

What made you want to become a copywriter?

Copywriting was not an aspiration for me until I became a copywriter. In fact, I didn't know what a copywriter was when I was hired as one! I was living in Tokyo and applied for a translation position at NTT, the largest telecom in the world. My Japanese was not quite up to par for the translation position, but instead they took me on as a copywriter, so I was working with English that had already been translated from the Japanese base.

I'm sure that starting work on the client side exclusively made my copywriting education infinitely easier in the beginning, since I was writing about one category of products. Working at an agency can be much more difficult as you have a wide variety of clients you may be writing for, and you must know each of their products and industries inside out. That depth of knowledge of the background of the topic you're writing about will make your writing much richer and more appealing to the audience, and you can concentrate on learning how to write for different media.

Case Study: Lisa Banks

With my background in marketing and a natural love for continually learning new things as well as a lifelong interest in writing, I quickly became very comfortable with copywriting. It's important to be interested in leaning how things work, asking questions that get to buyer motivations, not-so-obvious facts, and the bigger picture, so you can draw out the unique points for the product or service you're writing about. It's rarely as cut and dried as your client may think, as they are usually too close to be able to see it from the viewpoint of a potential customer. I loved the chance to look at ordinary things from different perspectives and find out what really makes one different from another.

What was your first assignment? How did you feel about it?

When I moved to the U.S., I was hired as a copywriter at an advertising agency where my first assignment was to write a press release announcing my appointment. I had never written a press release before! In my years in Tokyo, I was concentrating on copy for cell phone catalogs as well as technical writing for user manuals. But I had known that it would be important to learn more about different media, as the style of writing varies according to each. So, luckily I had been studying several copywriting books before taking the new position and was able to refer to some great advice on how to write and format a press release properly.

This is one thing that a copywriter must always do – keep learning about the media you are writing for, because copy for a corporate web site is going to be different from that used in a blog and different again from how you'll write a radio spot. Each medium is used by the audience in a different way, and you need to understand how to incorporate that into your writing style for each. With the evolution of the Internet, there are new things to consider constantly.

What do you know now that you wish you had known when you first started?

That every project would take longer than anticipated. When I first started freelancing, it was difficult to price work. The time you expect to invest forms the basis for your estimate, so you need to understand how long a project will take. Starting out, I was so happy to be hired that I often quoted too low. However, that didn't stop me from putting the effort into each job – in the beginning you need to focus on building a strong portfolio, so that is a form of payoff.

Until just last year, I used to estimate $350-$500/page for web copy. But copy is not always required in neat chunks by page. For example, you may also need to write copy for a Flash presentation and many sites display information dynamically based on the reader's actions, which means the same page may show different copy

Case Study: Lisa Banks

depending on whether they're logged in or not. In that case, you may be producing the same page with a few variations in copy. I also write copy for text that appears within order systems and shopping carts, which requires you follow the paths the customers can take and also make recommendations for usability. The conclusion I've come to is that Web copywriting must be accounted for on an hourly basis in order to accurately compensate for effort, though you still have to give the client an idea of how long you think it's going to take upfront.

Now as marketing director and lead copywriter with SEO Advantage, I often work with clients putting together proposals and pricing out our work. And because all our work is custom and I'm representing our team of designers, copywriters, and SEO associates, it's more complicated as I need to pull together estimates from each department.

What is the toughest copywriting challenge that you faced?

Some copywriters naturally do better writing for certain industries. I found one industry that I just did not enjoy writing for was construction. In the early 2000's in Florida when the building industry was flourishing, builders would engage the agencies where I worked to create their brochures and print ads.

For any copywriting project, a moment of "YES!" occurs when you realize the key points that are going to make the piece you are writing shine. You need to find why your client is different (better) than the other options and communicate that believably. Well, for the life of me, I could not find distinguishing features among any of the builders beyond very superficial "We'd like to emphasize this" type of direction. I was rarely satisfied with my work for builders because you could have changed the logo on the piece and it would have just as well suited the next builder to come along.

How does Web copywriting differ from traditional copywriting?

My focus is entirely on writing for the Web now, and you might very well fill an entire book with the ways in which Web copy differs from writing for offline media. But the more you try to detail the differences, the more you realize that a lot of copywriting basics are the same.

People don't read so much as scan copy online. While the same could be said of print copy, it's important to build scanning-friendly features into your online copy using subheadings, bullets, text treatments, and links. Short paragraphs and straightforward sentence structure helps make sure your point is understood. But once again, that can be true in any medium.

Case Study: Lisa Banks

To understand how writing for any medium differs, you need to understand how people use the medium. You need to understand how to write for radio if you're writing a radio commercial, in addition to understanding the product and the needs of people you're appealing to.

Consider that online readers are viewing the copy on their monitors instead of hard copy. They can't take it into the loo with them, and they're not likely to read your pages from top to bottom. They're looking for information, and they want to find it quickly, so you need to make it easy for different people to find the different information they need.

The fluid nature of the online medium means that a copywriter cannot consider his or her piece in isolation. Where a reader clicked from can play a role in how you present your copy, as in the case of writing landing pages for pay-per-click ads, for example. Usability and navigation of the entire web site plays a role – you will need to indicate links and "paths" a reader can follow.

With keyword studies and analytics, copywriters have at their disposal a lot more data that can be considered. The opportunities for personalization are much greater online, as you can display different copy based on the choices and actions of the reader if the client has programming resources. It's up to the copywriter to understand and suggest such techniques when they are appropriate. This means there's usually a lot more behind a successful online copywriting project than simply the words.

Even within copy for the Web, you are going to find different styles required for different online types of media. Your writing for your client's blog needs to take into account best practices for that medium, which differ from best practices for, say, writing paid search ads, landing pages, microsites, corporate web sites, press releases, directory listings, social media content, emails, and so on.

For example, it may be tempting to think you can just take a paragraph from your web site to submit for a directory listing, but dig a little deeper and you'll see there are best practices for preparing your listing copy that can really amplify the effects. Another example, it's common for copywriters to just throw in a subject line after writing an email, but research shows that's one of the more critical influences on whether the email is opened or not. Every detail of online copy has been studied, so copywriters have a big task to stay up on the latest research for the media they specialize in.

What is your biggest success? What copy have you crafted that you really loved?

Every project is different, and I take steps to ensure that every piece of copywriting

Case Study: Lisa Banks

I do is tailored to the client's requirements. But I love it when a client really wants to go for a distinct voice and the topic itself can be made exciting. A recent project that comes to mind involved writing a corporate web site for a software product that allowed people to access their files, contact databases, and also print documents from anywhere. The copy read like a casual chat you might have with a witty, knowledgeable person and it was easy to bring out the phenomenal benefits the service offered.

Another piece that stands out is a paragraph that was to appear on a brochure for a residential development deep in horse country. It was almost poetic, talking about the granddaddy oak trees and the sound of thundering hooves, etc. When I submitted the draft to the creative director at the agency, she was floored and insisted that not a word be changed. It's funny, but I have always found that type of copy easy to write. But bringing to life through words a seemingly boring industrial product is much more challenging, and I'm proud of being able to accomplish that personally. Writing for B2B clients isn't as glamorous at first glance, but it can be more rewarding.

What are the best tips you have for successful Web copywriting?

Keep learning. The Web is one medium that will always be changing, and there will never be a definitive set of rules. The best advice is to find sources that will provide you with updated research so you can make sure your writing evolves along with the medium and the way that people use it.

Do you feel that it is more important in copywriting to be creative or a salesman?

Certainly the creativity to seek out new ways to communicate and a solid understanding of what makes people buy will both be important qualities for a copywriter.

However, your two most important roles are as detective and communicator. First, you must find what needs to be said and the details that support that message, which is more a function of legwork and research, and then translate it into the language that will appeal to your audience.

What makes the Internet a great media for advertising?

Simply the prevalence of the Internet in people's lives. It has the potential to be much more targeted than TV, radio, and print, and its on-demand nature means that customers can find your advertising content whenever it is most relevant for them.

Which companies do you feel do best by advertising on the Internet?

Case Study: Lisa Banks

There is a place for every company to reach customers online, though the specific medium one uses may be different from another. For example, local targeting on Google will be more helpful than a broad SEO strategy for an independent plumber.

There are many companies that can thrive using only the Internet for promotion, most notably those with online stores or services. As an SEO, all of our promotion occurs online, and as a Web-focused freelance copywriter I used only my web site to draw leads. Even companies that have traditionally focused on branding through TV are pursuing aggressive online strategies, due to the importance of reaching audiences through the Internet.

Lisa Banks, MBA, is marketing director and lead copywriter for search engine optimization firm SEO Advantage. Learn more about the company's SEO and copywriting services at **www.seoadvantage.com** *and Lisa's background at* **www.lisabanks.com.** *Add her blog www.seo-e.com to your list of Web copywriting resources.*

Finding Copywriting Jobs

"Remember that you are needed. There is at least one important work to be done that will not be done unless you do it."
Charles L. Allen

You may be reading this book in an attempt to gain the skills you need to write better Web copy in the hopes of obtaining a job or improving your personal Web site. However, where do you look for copywriting jobs?

Help Wanted

The first place is the help wanted section of the local classifieds or the online version thereof. This way, you know there is a position that the company wants to fill, and you just have to be the best candidate to fill it.

Reading the help wanted section also gives you an opportunity to evaluate the company. If the help wanted ad lacks luster and excitement, you can always position yourself as what the company needs to help boost sales and creativity. If, on the other hand, the advertisement is creative, then you know you need to have the skills to match. Reading over the help wanted ads also gives you knowledge of what the company is looking for, because it often will say specific qualifications that you must possess. When reading over these qualifications, pick up on some of the key words that the company uses.

Key words to pay attention to as a copywriter:

Some — If the ad says they would like someone with some experience in a particular field, that means they are more willing to overlook the fact that you do not have extensive experience if you have a general knowledge.

Product — If the ad says they want to see product advertisements, this means you need to show actual advertisements that you have produced for a company.

Spec — If the ad says the business accepts spec ad advertisements in a portfolio, this means you do not need to have printed work for an actual company. If the company accepts spec work, it is more likely looking for, or willing to accept, new talent.

Thorough knowledge — No general knowledge of a particular subject will cut it here. This phrase is calling for someone with plenty of experience.

Finding a copywriting job can be a difficult task, because you are up against other people with talent and skill. However, the great thing about copywriting is that you do not necessarily need experience to land a job — you just have to be good.

What You Need to Get Started

If you have not already built a portfolio that showcases your skills, you need to begin working on one right away. All your potential employers will want to see examples of your work. This work does not have to have been previously published — though publication does help (just make sure to ask whether the company accepts spec work) — it just needs to be good work. If you do not have an extensive portfolio, you might consider freelancing to build up your portfolio. You may not make as much money as someone who has plenty of experience, but you will have the opportunity to work on projects to build your portfolio, which will allow you to make more money in the future.

Bright Idea

Find a mentor whom you trust. Have him or her critique your work so that you can improve.

If you want to write Web copy for advertisements, you need to show several different campaigns for a product or service in your portfolio. If you want to write Web copy for Web site content, you need to have several examples of Web sites that you have created for various products and services. If you wish to write online marketing pieces, you need examples of those, too. An advertising firm will want to hire a copywriter that possesses all these skills, so you might also want to make sure your portfolio encompasses diverse materials. Just remember to put your best work forward.

You may wish to include several examples of these to be a well-rounded Web copywriter and set yourself apart from the rest of the applicants. Having multiple examples shows you have consistent skills and that you can work in multiple platforms and media. Having multiple examples also helps an employer realize that it is your skill that is working and not someone else's creative idea (a teacher, a former employer, or a friend).

As an online copywriter, you must have your work samples available online. It is best for everyone to have an online portfolio. The best place to start is by creating your own Web site. Make sure there is a link to your portfolio, and provide good samples of your work.

Good examples of online portfolios for copywriters:

- www.justrightcopy.com

- www.wordstorm.co.uk

- www.writedirection.com

- www.marte-cliff.com

- www.hollywoodcopy.com

- www.SusanGreeneCopywriter.com

www.mikesmycopywriter.com

 www.copywritermike.com

You may also want to have a physical portfolio that you keep your samples in. This is good to present to your future employer when you go in for an interview. This should be in a neat binder or a portfolio book. These portfolios can be purchased at most office supply stores, such as Staples or Office Depot. Make sure that your portfolio looks professional and is neatly organized. You likely will have only one of these, so if a potential employer asks to hang on to it for a few days, make sure you get it back. The employer will understand.

A good remedy to an employer keeping your portfolio on hand is to have a "leave behind." You can make a smaller book with a few examples of your best work and allow the employer to keep it. You can also leave behind a CD of your portfolio, but sometimes these have a tendency to get misplaced and overlooked. It is better to have something that requires little effort to look through.

Always update your portfolio. Do not take an outdated portfolio to an interview. Keep coming up with new spec advertisements and building your portfolio to make it better. A portfolio created last year will not be as good as one you build next year. You should constantly be learning and practicing what you have learned.

After the Interview

Be sure to send a thank-you letter after the interview. Do not just have a generic thank-you letter that you send out to all potential employers you have interviewed with. Personalize each letter.

Maybe you noticed that the interviewer was a Miami Dolphins fan. You could make a comment about how you hope they have a great season. Another idea is to write about something that was discussed in the interview that you found intriguing. For instance, if the interviewer said you would be working on an account for JCPenny if you were to be hired, you could mention how you cannot wait for such an opportunity.

A thank-you letter gives you another opportunity to leave a good impression. Maybe the interview went poorly. A great thank-you letter can only help your case.

If It Is a No

Sometimes you get rejected. Many times you get rejected. Interviewing is about 90 percent rejection. You cannot let a little "no" get you down or make you feel as if you are no good at what you do. You cannot give up; you must keep trying. Keep building your portfolio.

If your heart was set on working for a particular company with which you interviewed, you can always ask the interviewer why you were not hired for the job. He or she may be able to provide you with advice that you can use for your next interview.

Another suggestion is to always keep in touch and use your interview as a networking opportunity. After all, someone thought highly enough of you to call you for the interview in the first place. Keep in touch by sending an e-mail every couple of months. Keep up-to-date about the company's business. If possible, share some of your new work and ask for guidance. This network will develop an "in" for you with the company, and perhaps the next time a position opens, you will already have one foot inside the door.

If It Is a Yes

Sometimes you get an offer. You beat out all the other applicants, and you have an employer that has enough confidence in your work to say, "Congratulations, you got the job."

It is vital to your success to keep improving. Learn as much as you can from the job. Find a mentor who will help you develop your creativity and salesmanship. Listen and learn. Never go into a job thinking that you know everything, because you will soon learn that you do not.

Bright Idea

Keep updating your portfolio with the work you are producing for the company.

After you have been at the company for a few months, take the time to evaluate the company. The company is evaluating you, so take the time to evaluate your work with them. You do not have to give the evaluation to your boss or have a conference with anyone about it. Just understand how you fit into the company and realize whether or not you are learning new things. At some point, you may decide to end your relationship, especially if you stop learning, if you develop a dislike for the company or for copywriting, or stop producing quality work. There is no sense in making yourself miserable; it will only affect the quality of your work.

Freelance

Sometimes you do not want to work for a big advertising company; instead, you want to work on the side as a freelance copywriter. This is a good alternative for someone who has other commitments or wants to build a portfolio.

If you want to freelance as a Web copywriter, you can register at a freelance Web site for a nominal fee and begin bidding on projects. Popular freelance Web sites include:

- elance.com

- guru.com

- odesk.com

- journalismjobs.com

You can also search for Web copywriting jobs on career-related Web sites, such as:

- Monster.com

- Careerbuilder.com

- Myspacejobs.com

- hotjobs.yahoo.com

You may have to look under "advertising" or "marketing" to find these jobs.

To become a freelance copywriter, you need the same skills and portfolio that you need when searching for a full-time job with a company. Possibly the most drastic difference in obtaining a freelancing job is the pay scale.

If you have read this book from the first chapter, you have read Case Studies by freelance copywriters that help explain why setting your pay scale is so important. If you price your work too low, people will not take you seriously. If you price your work too high, people may choose someone less expensive.

Do not go into a freelance job and bid on a project for too low a rate per hour. You have to calculate how much time will go into the work and set your rates accordingly. You need to be paid for the work that you do. Even though someone else may bid on a project with a drastically lower rate does not mean that person's work will be chosen over yours. A respectable company realizes it gets what it pays for in terms of copywriting.

To find a reasonable pay range, find other copywriters with skills and experience similar to yours and see what they are bidding on projects. You may want to start your bidding around that range. Of course, to be competitive, you may lower or raise the price; just make sure you are still making a profit from your work and you are not becoming greedy.

If you are new to copywriting, you may set your rates lower in the beginning, but remember to raise them as you acquire skills. If you freelance for a company for a while, do not think that just because you are a freelancer, you cannot ask for an increase in pay. A respectable employer will understand and evaluate your work performance accordingly. If a client finds you are doing a great job, it will not want to lose you and will likely either adhere to your request or strike a compromise with you.

Summary

There is a job out there for you that will help you develop your skills. If you are rejected at first, do not become discouraged. Someone once said that looking for a job was like practicing the art of rejection. Keep working to build your portfolio and better yourself at the craft of writing. Take freelance work to get your foot in the door, and start networking and developing your contacts.

Case Study: Dr. Debbie Treise

Dr. Debbie Treise knew that she wanted to be a copywriter because she did not like anything else in the advertising world. She also thought that creative advertising was fun. She has written mostly radio and TV commercials, because she loves to incorporate the use of sound effects. She thinks that commercials stimulate the imagination, and that is what makes commercials so much fun to create. She dislikes writing print copy, thinking it is the hardest media to write for. She thinks that the incorporation of video into the Internet makes for more interesting advertisements, because they allow for more creativity and provide a new way to reach an audience.

Dr. Treise began her career at a radio station. She wrote copy for the commercials and then also worked at selling airtime. She had her most embarrassing experience by not being prepared when she went to see a client. She did not realize the product it sold, because she says that it was something entirely different. When she was told it sold large bras, it was difficult for her to keep a straight face. She said she felt horrible afterward.

Case Study: Dr. Debbie Treise

Having worked in the copywriting field for many years, Treise has much advice for the novice copywriter. She says that rejection is a part of the job and that you should not "be married to your work." By this she means you cannot become too attached to anything because the client may not like it. She says that flexibility is a must in the copywriting world.

When asked whether you needed to be more creative or more of a salesperson with your copywriting work, Treise said it depended on where you were working. There will be times when you have to sell your work to your boss or to your client, but you always want to produce good creative material. She says that the smaller your place of work, the more things you have to do, which means you need to be equally creative and good at sales.

Dr. Treise says that her biggest accomplishment in life has been her son, but besides that, she likes seeing students succeed, especially when other people have told them they would fail. Her favorite commercial that she has written was an advertisement for K-Mart.

Dr. Treise has worked on advertising for KFC, K-Mart, Sears, and others. She currently is a professor and graduate studies chairman at the University of Florida. She also works as a freelance copywriter on occasion.

<u>Conclusion</u>

"There will come a time when you believe everything is finished. That will be the beginning."
Louis L'Amour

There is a plethora of Web copywriting jobs available and many suggestions on how to best write each of them. You glean more knowledge from each job you take and keep updating your portfolio to show your best work.

In the end, your work, along with the art director's, is what has the most visibility of any advertisement. No one sees the endless planning and behind-the-scenes work that goes into the production of advertising. They see only the advertisement, which is what you have written. Thus, the position of copywriter is one that is always scrutinized and under judgment from your bosses, your peers, and your audience. The criticism can be tough to take at times, but you should not let it discourage you. You are good at what you do and are working to become better. Someone believes in your work or you would not have been hired.

The criticism can be worth it when you are nominated and win awards for your efforts. Some of your worst pieces (to you) may be some of your best pieces. Always try to learn and better yourself. Failure is always on the path to success.

Bibliography

"Research to see what everybody else has seen, and to think what nobody else has thought."
Albert Szent-Gyorgyi

The Complete Guide to Google Advertising by Bruce C. Brown, Atlantic Publishing Co., 2007

The Secret Power of Blogging by Bruce C. Brown, Atlantic Publishing Co., 2007

The Copywriter's Handbook: A Step-by-Step Guide to Writing Copy that Sells Third Edition, by Robert W. Bly, Owl Books, Henry Holt & Company, 2005

The Online Copywriter's Handbook: Everything You Need to Know to Write Electronic Copy that Sells by Robert W. Bly, McGraw Hill, 2002

Hot Text: Web Writing that Works by Jonathan and Lisa Price, New Riders, 2002

Call to Action: Secret Formulas to Improve Online Results by Bryan and Jeffery Eisenberg with Lisa T. Davis, Future Now, 2005/06

The AdWeek Copywriting Handbook: The Ultimate Guide to Writing Powerful Advertising and Marketing Copy from One of America's Top Copywriters by Joseph Sugarman, John Wiley & Sons, Inc., 2007

Web Copy That Sells: The Revolutionary Formula for Creating Killer Copy Every Time by Maria Veloso, AMACOM, 2005

Letting Go of the Words: Writing Web Content that Works by Janice (Ginny) Redish, Morgan Kaufman Publishers, 2007

Author Biography

"Be the change you want to see in the world."
Mahatma Gandhi

Vickie Taylor is an award-winning writer and graphic designer who lives in Ocala, Florida. She holds a B.S. in advertising from the University of Florida, where she graduated summa cum laude. She enjoys reading, writing, design, laughing, and rescuing puppies. She is addicted to reality television, but she finds time to spend with family, friends, and her 2.5 "kids": Buddy, Reese, and Sammy. Her most notable "accomplishment" was auditioning for *American Idol Season 4*, though she was not a bad enough singer to see Simon Cowell. You can reach her by visiting **www.mytaylormadecreations.com** or by writing her at vickietaylor@mytaylormadecreations.com.